# Fish Heads and Folktales

## Reflections on Culture, Family, and Life from a Korean Adoptee

Peter M. Moran
(Kim Jai Chul)

The names of some of the individuals featured throughout this book have been
changed to protect their privacy.

Cover design by Nancy K. Pappas. See more of her work at http://nkpappasdesign.com.

*For my wife, son, parents, siblings, and in-laws.*
*You made this possible.*

# AUTHOR'S NOTE

There's a certain whimsical nature to family and culture. As a Korean boy adopted by Caucasian parents, my life's interesting twist came when I married into a Korean-American family. This story is a thirty-year journey, peppered with select moments of unclear personal identity that rises and culminates in a measure of acceptance and tapers to a more complete sense of inner peace. I like to think of it as ramen noodle soup for the soul.

I plan to stick around this earth for a while longer but also want to share some lessons I've already pulled from the universal experiences that make us all human—the things that impart on us a special brand of wisdom that can only be acquired by living through them—and so often turn out unexpectedly. Like a mother hen, I sat patiently on the idea to tell my story, and I'm grateful to the many people who helped make it a reality. I'm not a philosopher, but I hope these bits of wisdom will resonate with individuals and families from all backgrounds and walks of life. Most importantly, I hope these stories provide as much fun along the way to you as they did for me.

# Introduction

*All things have a beginning. Even great projects must start
with something, be it small or large.*
*—Korean Proverb*

## How It All Started

My mom and dad are mainstream Americans of German and Scot-Irish
descent. As a Korean adoptee, I grew up in places where I looked
different than most people around me, but I fit in culturally. When I
turned thirty, my life took a dramatic turn after I moved to New York
City and married into a Korean-American family. In my new city and
extended family, I attended a Korean church, shopped at Korean grocery
stores, and helped run my wife's Korean business. However, in an exact
reversal of situations, I often became a cultural outcast. It was perfect
irony. I finally lived and worked with people that I looked like, but many
of their customs were foreign to me, and more importantly, I didn't
speak Korean. I quickly learned the simplest way to handle a stranger
who assumes you speak Korean is to agree with everything they say,
bow repeatedly, and slowly back away until you're out of earshot.

Years ago, my love of writing inspired me to start a blog about my
life as a Korean adoptee living in America, my marriage into a Korean
family, and my ongoing quest to reconcile my dual identity: the one
given to me at birth, and the one I was raised to embrace. I blogged
about discovering my birth culture, both as a kid who spent many nights

reading popular Korean folktales in bed and as an adult face-to-face with a bowl of fish head soup. I eventually realized that a blog is a lot like a diet–it's easy to start but hard to maintain. So after a year, I closed the blog and conceived the idea to integrate my posts into a book.

In fall of 2011, I left my job at a large New York public relations agency and was looking for a new job when I decided to start this project. In between sending out my résumé and doing phone interviews, I found time to revisit my blog and figure out how to best turn it into a book. The room for improvement to what I considered a decent blog surprised me, but the foundation was there. I had content, time, and most importantly, my wife's full support. As Patricia O'Conner, my favorite author on the art of good writing, would say, *my egg was ready to hatch.*

## AN ADOPTION JOURNEY BEGINS

It wouldn't be out of the ordinary to see a new mother leave the hospital with an infant in her arms and a proud husband by her side. In fact, one would naturally expect it. However, after giving birth, a Korean woman named Hee Sook Kang left a Seoul hospital with nothing–nothing, that is, except faith the baby she left behind would find a loving family. She was probably young, single, and certainly didn't have money to care for a newborn. Whatever the reason, being part of a time and culture that

couldn't–and wouldn't–accept and support her, she gazed at her son one last time and vanished without a trace.

There was no way this woman could know exactly where and with whom her boy would end up. No way she could guess that more than thirty years later, he would return to Seoul on a

*Mom and Dad in October, 1967*

quest to find her and discover a clue that provided both satisfying answers and more tantalizing questions.

It was May 1, 1975, and South Korea was still an emerging country—not yet the prosperous nation it would eventually become. Half a world away in America's heartland, a young couple waited eagerly for good news about their application to adopt a child from overseas. Seven months later, the baby that Hee Sook abandoned left Korea for the United States. Soon after arriving, he became Peter Michael Moran, an all-American boy with an all-American story.

My parents both grew up in large families—my mom with four siblings, and my dad with five. My dad was born in Chicago, and my mom in New Ulm, a small city in rural Minnesota known as "The Polka Capital of the Nation." Aside from its annual Oktoberfest, New Ulm's claim to fame is the August Schell Brewing Company, founded in 1866 and the second oldest family-owned brewery in America. They met in St. Paul while my dad attended the College of St. Thomas, and my mom was minutes away at the College of St. Catherine. After my mom graduated, they got married on June 1, 1968 before the Marine Corps deployed my dad to Vietnam in 1969. "During the Vietnam War, you either enlisted and chose the military branch you wanted to join, or took a chance of peeling potatoes in the army," he explained after I once asked him why he joined the Marines. After my dad enlisted, he went on to Officer Candidate School and served as an F-4 Phantom RIO (radar intercept officer) stationed at Da Nang Air Base, eighty-five miles south of Vietnam's Demilitarized Zone. In 1970, my dad returned to the states and was stationed in Beaufort, South Carolina with my mom until his tour of duty ended in 1971. From there, my parents moved to St. Paul for a year before buying a house in Minneapolis. My dad started a career in accounting, and my mom, who had majored in chemistry, worked at a crime lab until my older sister Molly was born in 1973.

The Vietnam War continued for another five years after my dad returned home. During his service, my dad witnessed countless lost and orphaned Vietnamese children, and this moved him and my mom to grow their family through adoption. My parents originally wanted to adopt a child from Vietnam, as they were more familiar with that nation's history and heritage, but they were also open to adopt from Korea. In their application letter to the adoption agency, my dad explained: "We feel we could give our adopted child more love and understanding and a better environment for growth and self-fulfillment than he could have in an orphanage. Though we are not wealthy, we can offer a comfortable home, with educational and developmental opportunities for a growing child.

"We also feel that adopting a foreign-born child would expand our horizons, since we would wish to learn as much as possible about the child's country and heritage. Naturally, we would want our child to know about his heritage and be proud of it.

"We would very much like to have a mixed-race family. We feel that the only way to have peace in the world is for people to understand each other. By adopting a foreign-born child, we could perhaps bring about more understanding, at least among our family and friends."

A month after Hee Sook left her baby to the hands of fate, my parents received the news they had long hoped for in letter dated May 30, 1975 from the Holt Adoption Program.

*Dear Friends:*
*Congratulations! We are pleased to tell you that you have been accepted as an adoptive family.*
*As soon as we have a child for whom we feel you would be the right parents, we will notify your agency and send all the information we have. Your caseworker will help you notify your agency and send all the information we have...*

In a placement agreement dated June 5, 1975, my parents were notified that case number K-7799, Kim, Jai Chul, would soon join them and their two-year-old daughter.

In the meantime, I was placed in a foster home in Seoul. My foster parents, a young couple with an eight-year-old son and ten-year-old daughter of their own, cared well for me while I waited to emigrate. My official record notes:

"Jai Chul had jaundice at the time of placement and looked yellow, but he has recovered completely now thanks to his foster mother's good care since placed. He has been growing well without any troubles recently and is normally developed both in physical and emotional areas for his age."

*My adoption file photo*

Seven months later on December 10, 1975 at 5:30 p.m., Western flight 526 touched down at Minneapolis-St. Paul International Airport where my mom, dad, and older sister waited to welcome me into their family. An escort from Holt International Children's Services accompanied me from Korea, and I'm guessing she was probably relieved to be on the ground after hours in the air with an infant. My mom said I was very fussy and needed a diaper change when I arrived.

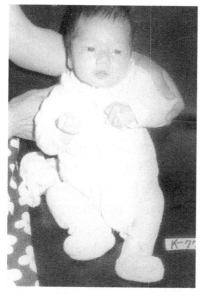

*Kim, Jai Chul in 1975*

My adoption day was one of several more to come for my family, and over the years, my parents went on to adopt three other children.

When I was four, my younger sister Lia became part of the family. Lia was born in the city of Bhagalpur, India, and was originally named Deepti. She was taken as a baby by train to an orphanage in Delhi run by the Missionaries of Charity. This order of nuns is the order of Mother Teresa, who often visited this orphanage, and cared deeply for all the poor around her. Lia contracted meningitis and had some early paralysis and delays, but recovered from that and lived with many other children in the orphanage.

All adoptions from the Missionaries of Charity orphanages were facilitated by a small group of volunteers, including a number of flight attendants who escorted children to their families throughout the world. An Indian American woman who lived in Washington, D.C. was the U.S. liaison with the orphanages, and suggested placements for available children with families.

My parents received information about Lia in 1978 and requested medical tests to be run because of her meningitis and some other health concerns. At that time, medical information was minimal, as the orphanage had very limited resources. Lia was just over two years old when she arrived to our family in spring of 1979. An asthma attack shortly after she arrived landed her in the hospital, but she adapted physically to her environment and life with her new brother and sister.

Three years later in 1982, my younger, and only brother, Nick came into our lives. I share much more about this special kid later on.

I was fifteen when my youngest sister Jenn joined the Moran clan in 1989. Before Jenn came, my parents called a family meeting so we kids could discuss how we felt about a new sibling. Jenn, who is mixed Korean and Puerto Rican, was born in Seoul and originally named Eun Ju. She lived with her dad and "grandma," a woman Jenn recently discovered was actually a close friend of her biological grandma who had raised her father.

When Jenn was four, she and her dad moved to Colorado Springs on an Amerasian Visa through the Pearl S. Buck Foundation, an organization that helps mixed-race Asians come to the U.S. Jenn and her dad lived with their sponsoring family for a year, but were eventually evicted due to her father's alcohol abuse. They moved to the Denver area, and her dad moved Jenn around with several different families, until he eventually sought to have her adopted. Jenn came to live with us in a foster situation and was seven when her father terminated his parental rights. My parents officially adopted her in 1990.

# THE EARLY YEARS

*My sister Molly and me*

By most accounts, my family life was normal—if there is such a thing. We were a modern middle-class family but also traditional, and this came from how both of my parents were raised. My parents instilled in us the importance of honesty, education, saving money, and taking personal responsibility for our actions. Most importantly, they taught us the virtue of hard work. Even "Take Your Kid to Work Day" for school wasn't a free day for me. I remember when my dad took me to with him to work when I was in fifth grade. Right when we got to his office, he sat me down at a desk and placed a pad of graph paper, a pencil, and a ruler in front of me. "I've been planning to rearrange my office," he informed me. "Since you like art and design, I want you to lay out a few different floor plans." I'm sure there were a couple other projects during the day, and I learned early on that work is work.

My parents didn't punish us unjustly, but they did let us experience both the natural and their imposed consequences of our decisions. For that, I'm grateful. Parents that let their kids get away with murder don't do them any favors and only set them up for bigger shock down the road. I've hardly been Saint Peter in my life, but I shiver at the thought of what I could have turned out like but for the grace of God and the loving discipline of two parents.

It's sad that the family dinner has largely slipped away as a societal tradition. My family wasn't the Cleavers, but we did sit down to eat meals together at the table, not in front of the TV or on the go. We didn't answer phone calls during meals, or leave until our mom or dad excused us. Table manners were of utmost importance. "Put your napkin on your lap, keep your elbows off the table, and don't talk with your mouth full," our parents would remind us. One could be sent away from a meal for laughing too much, which meant we kids would spend a lot of time trying to make each other laugh and get in trouble. I was the master of this—especially when our parents had opera on for dinner music. When Mom and Dad weren't looking, I quietly lip-synced in dramatic fashion, to which Jenn always ended up bursting with laughter.

My parents only allowed us to turn on the TV with permission, and only during evenings and Saturday morning. In Minnesota, my sister Molly and I loved going over to play with friends down the block because we'd hang out in their basement and watch episode after episode of *Gilligan's Island* and *Scooby Doo*. Sneaking TV at our house became an art—a well rehearsed, perfectly timed, and coordinated routine. In our home in Billings, Montana, the TV was downstairs, but there was a clear line of sight through the floor vent in the living room upstairs. When our parents were away, my siblings and I would watch TV, and one of us would stay upstairs on "parent patrol" while watching TV through the vent. When the designated person heard the garage door opening, he or she would signal the alert. "Mom and Dad are home!" the lookout person would bark. Then, someone who was downstairs would quickly turn off the TV and everyone would scramble away and pretend as if we'd been reading or doing something else constructive the whole time. In the next home we lived in, my brother Nick and I had an ongoing game of Monopoly set up and stashed under the family room couch. We'd watch TV, and any time Mom would come around, we'd quickly turn it off, slide the board out from its hiding spot, and continue our game.

Besides sneaking TV, my siblings and I did normal kid stuff— we took piano lessons, played soccer, studied at night, did chores on Saturdays, and went

*Celebrating Lia's 6ᵗʰ birthday*

to church on Sundays. We took summer vacations together, played together, and like all typical brothers and sisters, we had our share of fights. Our mom let us settle our own disputes. "Fight if you want," she would say. "Just clean up your own blood." Like all brothers and sisters, we had a pecking order, and grief naturally rolled downhill. Unfortunately for my youngest sister Jenn, she usually bore the brunt of the harassment, teasing, and pranks—and there were plenty.

My siblings and I had two outdoor chores we all despised. Weeding the garden and cleaning up after the dog. A summer afternoon that my family still recounts during gatherings is when my mom told all of us kids to go outside to scoop up the poop that our dog had left scattered all over the yard. Not wanting to waste a beautiful afternoon on such an unpleasant chore, the older of us kids tried to convince Jenn, who was maybe seven or eight, that she had to do it all by herself. "If you don't clean up the whole yard by yourself, Mom is going to send you to

'Pooper-Scooper Camp'—a place where you and other bad kids will do nothing else for an entire week except pick up dog poop," I threatened. The gag worked—only too well. Jenn broke into tears. "Mom!" she wailed and ran inside to verify this evil threat. The reset of us quickly got to work, knowing that Mom would be out any second to see what was going on. We waited, but nothing. It turns out that after hearing our ludicrous claim, our mom was unable to yell at us because she couldn't stop laughing at the thought of a camp where all you packed was a shovel and week's supply of plastic bags. Jenn will never let us live that one down.

I have forgotten a lot of other incidences and only remember when Jenn brings them up. Like when she reminded me about the time I had once hung her by her overall straps to a tree in our yard while our brother Nick shot her with crabapples from a homemade slingshot. I guess it's not surprising how much better the victim always remembers these things.

Overall, I had a positive childhood and adoption experience, but I don't take either for granted. From the beginning, my parents worked hard to balance my Western upbringing with trips to Korean heritage camps, occasional healthy portions of fragrant kimchee (spicy fermented cabbage) and lively rounds of "Santoki" (a popular Korean children's song about a mountain rabbit), and for this, I'm grateful. While cultural trappings didn't solve everything, they were an essential part of my parents' effort to help me learn about and embrace my Korean roots and adoption.

In 1979, my parents took me to the courthouse to become a naturalized U.S. citizen. They decided to wait until I was old enough to at least somewhat understand what was going on and to be a part of it. I don't really remember that day, but I still have the form letter the White House sent congratulating me on becoming an American. The last paragraph reads: "Naturalized citizens from all lands have made significant contributions to the betterment of our nation. I am sure that you will follow in this tradition and firmly resolve to do your part in making it an even more wonderful place in which to live.

Sincerely, Jimmy Carter." It was a lofty mandate for a four-year-old, and honestly, I'm still working on it.

Back in elementary school, we started each day by reciting the pledge of allegiance followed by singing "My Country, 'Tis of Thee."

> *My country, 'tis of thee,*
> *Sweet land of liberty,*
> *Of thee I sing.*
> *Land where my fathers died,*
> *Land of the pilgrims' pride,*
> *From ev'ry mountainside*
> *Let freedom ring!*
> *My native country, thee,*
> *Land of the noble free,*
> *Thy name I love.*
> *I love thy rocks and rills,*
> *Thy woods and templed hills;*
> *My heart with rapture thrills,*
> *Like that above.*

As I got a little older, I recall thinking to myself: *This isn't where MY fathers died. This isn't my native country, is it?* Don't get me wrong, I was and always will be a proud American. I consider my citizenship a gift and wouldn't give it up for anything, but I did think about things like this from time to time.

In an effort to leave me with some connection to Korea, my dad requested that I retain dual citizenship. After I was naturalized, he wrote a letter to the Holt Adoption Agency: "When you notify the Korean authorities of our son's naturalization, we would like you to request that he be allowed to maintain his Korean citizenship until he reaches the age of his majority." My parents received the following reply: "As per your request concerning Peter's retaining Korean citizenship until he reaches the age of majority is beyond our control. Once he is naturalized, he can no longer be under the country's citizenship unless it is specifically prescribed by the laws of the country concerned. As far as I know, there is no such Korean law."

My naturalization letter also included a typed note at the top.

*Dear Mr. and Mrs. Moran,*
*I'm very sorry that it has taken so long to acknowledge the receipt of Peter's naturalization and to answer your request that Korea be notified that you would like him to retain his Korean citizenship. I asked Mr. David Kim of our office about this latter concern. He advises that when Peter is 18, he can re-apply for Korean citizenship.*

From the time my parents adopted me, they plugged themselves into the international adoption community in Minneapolis and became close with several families that also had adopted children. Like most kids, I didn't sort my friends by race. I also didn't obsess about being an Asian raised by white parents. Sure, I saw almond-shaped eyes and jet-black hair when I looked in the mirror; however, I only thought of my body as a shell. I was aware that I looked different, but I didn't want to be different. I was, as many Korean adoptees affectionately call themselves, a Twinkie—yellow on the outside, white on the inside.

When I was seven, my dad worked as an accounting manager for a subsidiary of Burlington Northern Railroad. I still remember the night he and my mom called our whole family into the living room. Normally when our parents called everyone together, it meant one of us was in trouble—and usually only one of us knew for what. Not this time. This news was much bigger than cookies missing from the cookie jar. Dad explained that his job was moving to a place called Billings, Montana, and as a result, so were we. Like many smaller U.S. cities, Billings wasn't very diverse. The 2010 census reported just 0.7 percent of the city's 104,170 people as Asian—and I don't imagine it was much higher in 1980. However, for the most part, I only thought about my differentness if someone else pointed it out. One day in second grade, a classmate turned to me as we stood in line for recess and asked about my Asian features. "Why is your face so flat?" she asked with childlike innocence and lack of social grace.

*My face is flat?* I thought to myself.

It hadn't occurred to me. I brought my hands up and felt my face to confirm her observation. Her question caught me off guard and left me speechless. For a moment, it was as if I were actually a white kid trying to explain a physical deformity. Briefly stumped, I answered her as a matter of fact. "I don't know." My explanation didn't satisfy either of us, but my wit wasn't sharp enough to deliver a snappy retort, nor did I know enough about physical anthropology to give a serious answer.

However, being adopted did have some advantages in grade school. For example, show and tell was always a breeze, and I never struggled to find something to bring and talk about when my turn came around. My Korean folktale books and other cultural trinkets made great conversation pieces, and explaining my adoption and family to others eventually became a source of pride.

## MIDDLE YOUTH AND BEYOND

When I was nine, my dad's job moved again. This time we relocated to Littleton, Colorado, a suburb south of Denver. Before we moved, my parents had gone ahead to house hunt, and they returned with some good news for us kids. "Our new house has a big hole in the backyard," my dad hinted. None of us got it at first.

"The hole is filled with water," my mom added, another clue to the mystery. We finally realized they were talking about an in-ground swimming pool, and it somewhat softened the blow of having to leave our friends and classmates again.

Our new community was more diverse than Billings, but ignorant questions and comments didn't disappear completely. In middle school, classmates commonly asked if I knew kung fu or karate, and in high school, someone once pointedly observed that I spoke English really well. I credit that mastery to a lifetime of speaking the language–along with a little help from Hooked on Phonics. Both in middle and high school, I always ended up befriending the few other racial minorities in my classes. I'm not really sure why; I didn't do it consciously, but somehow it always happened.

In addition to exposing me to as much Korean culture as possible, my mom tried her best to give me a positive view of adoption. I had a childhood friend who was also adopted, and we'd often go see movies together at the local theater. I was fifteen when Universal Pictures released *Problem Child* in 1990, and both of our moms told us we weren't allowed to go see it. This dismal comedy's basic plot revolves around an abandoned boy who wreaks havoc and destruction as he's repeatedly rejected and returned to his orphanage thirty times until a shady adoption agent played by Gilbert Gottfried finally pushes him off on a naive, desperate and unsuspecting couple. The entire movie is built around the boy's cartoonish pranks and acts of revenge whenever he doesn't get his way.

I found out later that many people in the adoption community boycotted the movie because of the way it portrayed adopted kids as, well, problem children with attachment disorders and, worse, veiled it beneath lowbrow slapstick comedy. Like all teenage boys who didn't listen to our moms, we snuck off and watched it anyway once it hit the discount theatre. More than twenty years later, it's still ninety minutes of my life and a dollar I wish I had back.

My siblings and I played soccer during our childhood. I was never that good, but I joined the team in high school my freshman year. I was a fast runner, which made up for my lack of other fundamental athletic skills. That season, my teammates nicknamed me Fuji due to the flying high kicks I displayed while trying to intercept soccer balls in midair. I assume Fuji was a reference to Japan's famous mountain and, by cultural proxy, was somehow linked to karate. The name stuck, and although everyone knew I was Korean, I dismissed it as a case of poor geography skills. Fuji was actually just one of my nicknames in high school. The other one was Chewbacca. This came about from me trying to sport a mullet with thick Asian hair that stuck straight up when short. Imagine a black Q-tip on top and shoulder length hair in back.

Although I'd never make the varsity squad, I stuck with it. My sophomore year, I got really brave and decided to wrestle. People weren't lining up to join the wrestling team—the workouts were hard and practice was a dreaded part of every day. So, I made the team and felt pretty good about myself.

As part of my continued adolescent quest to be cool, I decided to move up in the world and try out for the football team my junior year—much to my mom's dismay. Let's just say I was no Hines Ward—the wide receiver born to a Korean mother and African-American father, who played fourteen seasons for the Pittsburgh Steelers and was the first Korean-American to win the Super Bowl MVP Award. I quickly discovered the consequences of being one of the smallest and most inexperienced players on the team, but again, I was determined and stuck with it for a season. I still recall one time the team was on a bus waiting to leave for a road game. We were parked in front of the school, and a group of Japanese foreign exchange students came out of the cafeteria. One of the team's co-captains, who was sitting right behind me, looked out the bus window and joked, "Hey look, guys! It must be chink-o de Mayo!" A few people laughed, and I just pretended I didn't hear the comment. I thought to myself, *Doesn't he realize I'm sitting right here?*

High school presented a few other rough patches, but I mostly escaped the relentless teasing and daily fights some of my other adopted friends around the country endured. One summer I attended a camp for Korean adoptees, and one of the guys told a group of us that his classmate was always trying to pick a fight with him. One day in the hall, the bully shoved and called him "a walking egg roll." The antagonist ended up getting the fight he expected, but also something he didn't—a broken nose.

The summer before I left for college, my university assigned random roommates to all incoming freshmen. I still lived in Denver, and Chris, the stranger I spent my first semester crammed into two hundred square feet with, hailed from upstate New York. Before classes began, I called him to break the ice. We discussed our planned majors, the stuff we needed for our room, and other typical get-to-know-you chitchat.

That fall, I moved into our dorm before Chris arrived, and the puzzled look on his face when we finally met in person burned itself into my memory. As he glanced around to make sure he had the right room, I could almost hear his thoughts. *Who the heck are you? I spoke to Peter Moran on the phone. Funny, you don't look white.*

"Where's the party?" he asked casually after he quickly recovered from his initial surprise and tossed his bags on the floor. As if I were back in second grade attempting to explain my face, I replied with the same unvarnished truth.

"I don't know."

In the end, everything turned out okay, and we became friends. It's not that Chris disliked Asians—far from it. He just rightfully assumed I was white and also cool enough to have a pulse on the campus party scene. Honestly, based on Chris's name and our conversations, if he hadn't been white, I would've been as equally surprised.

After graduation, I had no idea what I wanted to do besides get out of my college town and get a fresh start. I thought about where I wanted to go, and eventually set my heart on either Los Angeles or San Francisco. I honestly don't know why I chose those two cities, or even California for that matter—maybe they just seemed like cool places to be for a naive young art major with a progressive mindset. So, I hauled my stuff back to my parents' house, packed a bag, and bought a one-way plane ticket to San Francisco. I transferred from my college job at Kinko's to a San Francisco store, so I had a job but no solid long-term plan. Still, I suppose that was part of the post-college self-discovery experience I desired. "I can't believe you're doing this without a plan," my mom said on the way to the airport. "You don't even have a place to stay."

"Don't worry, I'll make it," I said, not sure if I was trying to reassure her or myself.

I didn't know a single soul when I arrived in San Francisco. After landing at the airport, I took a bus into the city, got off somewhere downtown with no idea where I was going to stay. After wandering around like I knew where I was going, I checked into one of those rent-by-the-week places in the Tenderloin district—an area of town with a long-standing seedy reputation. The drug dealers, prostitutes, and other colorful characters that inhabited the district quickly opened my eyes to a world beyond suburban America and the shelter of academia. I expected the city by the bay to have a fresh ocean breeze scent but instead was hit with the smell of urine and body odor—a smell that anyone who lives in a big city and rides the subway knows well. It was a bit of a culture shock, but looking back, it provided the new and exciting environment I craved.

After an extensive but unfruitful search for a permanent place to live in San Francisco, I moved across the Bay to a tiny studio in Oakland. I commuted to and from San Francisco every day and eventually started to look for a new job. As I went on interviews, I'm certain I caught a few human resource personnel off guard. After all, my résumé didn't give any clues about my ethnicity and they probably had no idea that I was Asian before I showed up. Somehow, Peter Moran, Bachelor of Fine Arts, conjures up quite a different picture than, say, Peter Kim, BS Applied Mathematics.

I loved the San Francisco Bay Area and still do, but the cost of living rose rapidly, and my income didn't. I refused to rent a dusty storage space beneath someone's staircase to live in, so three years after I planted myself in the Golden State, I pulled up roots and headed back to Colorado.

In 2003, I applied to graduate school to pursue an MBA. It was one of the most challenging things I've done. Being an art major, I didn't know a balance sheet from a hole in the ground. Every semester, I had at least one professor who seemed perplexed that my name didn't match my face. "I'm Irish, I swear," I usually quipped to gloss over the issue. Now, I look back and ask myself, *Should it have surprised me that people would expect someone with my last name to look different than I did?* Probably not. Heck, I should have just been satisfied when people pronounced my name correctly as More-ann instead of Moron.

# LIFE LESSONS

## A Real Family Is Defined by Love, Not Genes

*It is not flesh and blood but the heart*
*that makes us fathers and sons.*
*—Friedrich Schiller*

*My sister, Lia (left), brother, Nick (center),*
*and sister, Molly (right)*

There aren't many things that bring a family together more than an annual vacation. Most summers, we packed our camping gear and ourselves into the family Suburban and headed to the great outdoors. Think *National Lampoon's Vacation*—except that Colorado campground where the Griswolds stop on the way to Wally

World theme park was our actual destination. Living in Montana and Colorado afforded us convenient access to some of the most scenic parts of the country like Glacier National Park, Yellowstone, Rocky Mountain National Park and the Grand Canyon.

This was long before the days of Nintendo Game Boys and minivans equipped with entertainment systems. We only had our Walkmans for as long as the batteries lasted, and then it was on to travel bingo and games my mom just made up to entertain us.

"The first kid to spot a grizzly bear wins twenty-five cents," she offered in an attempt to keep us quiet and occupied. During these trips, the only thing more certain than nobody spotting a grizzly from the car was that my motion sickness would kick in somewhere along the climbing switchbacks of the Continental Divide, or a long stretch of interstate across the Great Plains. My mom kept a plastic dishpan at the ready for instances when my dad couldn't pull off to the side of the road quickly enough. To this day, I still can't eat blueberry malts from Dairy Queen.

Camping was fun, but it was also a practical way for my parents to take our family of seven on vacation without breaking the bank. For them, having to deal with a week of carsick kids and an occasional peed-in sleeping bag was still better than dipping into their retirement fund to stand in line at Disneyland or brush shoulders with the jet set in Aspen for few days. I don't blame them. In fact, when we lived in Colorado, I recall only skiing once or twice with my family, and that was because my younger brother participated in a handicapped ski program. People always seem surprised that I didn't grow up skiing. "What, you lived in Denver and you didn't ski?" is a typical reaction when I tell someone I'm not a skier. "Does everyone who lives in Los Angeles surf?" is my best response, which usually elicits a "good point." I never felt deprived. Besides, as a kid, there was something comforting about gathering as a family around a campfire to roast marshmallows and snuggling into our tent to the relaxing cadence of cricket chirps.

Whether we knew it or not, the seemingly simple act of camping was also a good family bonding experience. Sure, we all griped at times, but it forced us to work together, from pitching our monster-sized family tent in the dark to venturing in pairs through the night to outhouses crawling with daddy longlegs and other things only our imaginations could conjure up.

We took many of these camping trips before my parents adopted my youngest sister Jenn, so for many years, it was just four of us kids. During one trip to Glacier National Park, we were enjoying the view at a natural overlook and even spotted a fox trotting across the field below when an older couple approached us and began to chat with my parents.

"What a beautiful family you have," the woman exclaimed.

She asked about us kids and our adoptions, which all seemed fairly normal. Usually, fellow tourists hand you their camera and ask you to take *their* picture, but in a strange turn of events, she asked if she could take a picture of us (with her camera). Perhaps caught off guard, my mom agreed, and we gathered together to pose for her snapshot.

I know this couple's reaction to our family and odd request was innocent, but I'm still curious about what that woman did with the photo. Did she paste it into their vacation scrapbook next to pictures of bison and mountain goats? Did she create slides of her photos and show her friends a sighting more rare than a grizzly bear?

Over the years, I've talked with countless adoptees and adoptive parents about their experiences being part of a multiracial family, and many told stories that are similar to mine. Like the couple at Glacier, many people inquire in an innocent and even complimentary way. Others just make blatantly ignorant comments.

To adoptive parents: "Are they *really* yours?"

To adoptees: "Do you know your *real* parents?"

To an adoptee's sibling: "She isn't your *real* sister, right?"

I'm sure people gave our family more curious looks than any of us ever noticed, but for some reason, the Glacier vacation story stuck in my head. I try not to remember it as the day we became a tourist attraction, but instead, one of those moments that made me understand what a special (and real) family I'm part of. However, even with this realization, the unknown identity of my biological parents and uncertainty of my own openness to adopt continued unresolved for many more years.

# If You Have Old Clothes, You Can Make a Halloween Costume

*I'll bet living in a nudist colony takes
all the fun out of Halloween.*
—*Unknown*

*Nick and Jenn all dressed up for Halloween*

When we were young kids, if we wore a hole in pair of jeans, my mom would sew a patch onto it, and the pants would eventually get passed down to the next oldest kid in line. My family wasn't poor, but we certainly didn't wear brand name clothes or fashions. However, that didn't stop me from trying to create my own. The mid to late 80s were an era of bleached hair and denim. It was the height of glam rock and heavy metal, and for me, a pair of bleached jeans meant looking like a rock star or one of the cool kids at school. For my mom, it meant a destroyed and wasted pair of pants. One day after school, I snuck down to the laundry room on a mission to create my own pair of custom Levis. The only problem with my plan and something I didn't think about ahead of time is that bleach smells—a lot. It was only a matter of time before my mom caught a whiff and came downstairs to investigate. "What in blazes do you think you're doing?!" she yelled as I stood there with the jeans all covered with bleach streaks. I had no answer, no justification, and no way out. I don't remember my punishment, but I'm certain I didn't get any new jeans for a long time.

Now, as an adult, I'm amazed at the different types of jeans that have come in and out of fashion over the years. First it was skinny, then baggy, then back to skinny again. For a while, the craze was designer jeans with pre-torn holes and even paint drips. It baffles me that people will actually pay money to buy "new" jeans that are already destroyed. I've often thought of starting a line of dress shirts and ties that come with pre-made ink and mustard stains for busy executives that don't have time to wait. It hasn't panned out yet. When I find myself getting to critical though, I just think back to the 80s and remember that what's cool is cool—it doesn't have to make any sense.

Around the same time I thought bleached jeans were cool, my mom signed me up for Tae Kwon Do at the local recreation center. This was one of many things my parents did to help me connect with my Korean heritage. I was a relatively shy kid and wasn't comfortable in unfamiliar situations, so I wasn't thrilled at first. The instructor was white, and I was actually the only Korean kid in the class. Ironically, this was where I first learned to count to ten and some other basic Korean words. I don't remember exactly why, but I only made it to yellow belt (one rank above white) before my mom pulled me out of the class.

A couple years later, she enrolled me in a traditional Korean Tae Kwon Do studio. I felt like Daniel in the *Karate Kid* must have after he went from YMCA classes to learning from Mr. Miyagi. My new instructor was a stern old Korean Tae Kwon Do master who practiced old-school discipline and didn't tolerate any disobedience or horseplay. After I joined the class, he gave me an introductory lecture. "You have to start over as a white belt so you can learn Tae Kwon Do the *real* way," he explained. It was slightly accusatory–as if I had grown up in a Korean family, I'd already have learned the *real* way. He had two rules. First, we all had to address him as sir, and second, we had to bow anytime we greeted him. If we forgot to bow, it was trouble.

I could comply with his philosophy and teaching style–all except for the part about not tolerating goofing off. I always partnered to spar with another boy about my age, and we would always end up laughing and clowning around. "What's so funny?" the instructor would yell while hitting the back of our hands. "Both of you give me twenty-five pushups!"

"Yes sir," we'd both chant while trying hard not to giggle.

I persevered, though and eventually received my green belt (two ranks above white), but this was as far as I ever got. My parents eventually pulled me out because my math grades were so bad, and I never took up Tae Kwon Do again. Nevertheless, I did find one final use for my uniform before I put it away forever.

When my siblings and I were kids, October 31 was extra special to our family because it's also my mom's birthday. On Halloween, we'd eat birthday cake, my mom would open her gifts, and then we'd get dressed up in our costumes and head out for trick or treating.

My mom assembled most of our Halloween costumes with items she pulled from boxes of play dress-up clothes we had stashed in the basement. These clothes were a mish mash of items from our grandparents, some of my dad's old clothes, and bits and pieces my mom had picked up over the years at rummage sales and bargain stores. One Halloween, she took my dad's old fighter pilot helmet, an orange jumpsuit, made a light saber from a toilet paper roll, and presto—I was Luke Skywalker in X-wing fighter gear.

My mom is also a whiz on the sewing machine. One year, she made these great Miss Piggy and Kermit the Frog costumes for herself and my dad. My older sister and I got several good secondhand uses out of the costumes and even won first prize when a local movie theater hosted a Halloween party and costume contest for kids. Even my mom's parents dressed up as the famous Muppet duo one Halloween.

The years I took Tae Kwon Do were some of the last few times I dressed up for Halloween as a kid. Copying my mom's resourcefulness but lacking in creativity, I realized that my uniform could easily double as a Halloween costume. My easy and uninspired garb didn't win any awards, but I also didn't spend five minutes trying to peel off a giant banana outfit when I had to pee.

Perhaps my lack of effort violated the spirit of Halloween, and you may even ask if my Tae Kwon Do uniform even qualified as a Halloween costume. It did. I'll set the record straight now and explain that I dressed up as the only Korean in history to never advance past green belt for getting poor grades in math. If that's not scary, I don't know what is.

# WHEN YOU LIKE A GIRL, IT HELPS TO HAVE A CAR (OR A BOAT)

*Everything in life is somewhere else,*
*and you get there in a car.*
*—E. B. White*

A t some point in life, almost all of us fall into a romance that was just never meant to be. Sometimes it happens in high school, sometimes in college. Regardless of when, the experience always seems the same. When we lived in Colorado, my mom got involved with an adoptive families organization that launched an annual Korean Heritage Camp. The camp eventually grew to become the largest of its kind in the country. It's still going strong more than twenty years later and attracts adoptive families and guests from all over the world. I looked forward to attending this camp every year, and it's where I met some of my closest friends, both as a camper and later as a counselor.

The summer after I graduated from high school, I met a girl at the camp who was also adopted from Korea. I don't remember exactly how we first started hanging out, but we spent the entire three days together through Tae Kwon Do lessons and Korean cooking classes, and I had a crush on her long after camp ended. We wrote and called each other the rest of the summer, which now seems ridiculous considering we lived fifteen miles apart. But I didn't have a car, so fifteen miles may as well have been fifteen hundred.

That fall, I left for college, and she started her senior year in high school. After I moved away, I still hadn't let her know that I liked her as more than a friend, so that September, I hatched a plan to show up out of the blue as a birthday surprise. Her favorite music was reggae; so I picked out one of Bob Marley's biographies as a gift. A book seemed fitting, as she had given me a copy of *The Alchemist*, a fable about following your dream. So, with a gift and a dream, I was all set to go back to Denver. However, I had the same problem in college that I did the previous summer: no car. "I have to get down to Denver to see this girl, but I don't have a way to get there," I explained my predicament to Chris, my roommate.

"You really like this girl, huh?" I'll take you down if it means that much to you," he replied.

"You're not suggesting what I think," I asked suspiciously. What better way to complete my half-baked idea than to ride seventy miles down the interstate on the back of my roommate's motorcycle? Chris's bike wasn't a Harley cruiser with a big rear seat and back rest—no, this was a "hold on for dear life, try not to burn my leg on the exhaust pipe while gnats hit me in the face at eighty miles per hour" motorcycle. As we sped down I-25, every eighteen-wheeler that passed us convinced me we were going to blow off the road like a fly that accidentally gets too close to the front of a box fan.

By some miracle, we made it to Denver in one piece and found my friend's house. "We'll what are you waiting for? Go ring the bell," Chris prompted me as we stood on the sidewalk.

"Okay, I'm going," I replied nervously. I didn't even know if she was home, and the sheer foolishness of what I was doing suddenly hit me as I walked up her family's front steps. Chris and I were prepared to leave if she wasn't around or couldn't hang out, but by chance, she was home feeling sick but was still thrilled to see me—wind-burned face, head of tussled hair, frozen boogers, and all. We hung out until her parents got home. "Hey, Mom, look who it is!" my friend exclaimed. I'd also met her mother at the Korean Heritage Camp, and she was also happy to see me. My friend's mom went all out to make us feel welcome and even prepared Japanese tempura for dinner.

Later, my friend picked up one of her girlfriends, and the four of us went out. That night, we ended up sneaking into Red Rocks Amphitheatre, which is an open-air concert venue built into the surrounding natural red sandstone. It was a perfect early autumn night with a cool and clear star-filled sky. We all had a good time talking and climbing on the rocks, and we even got chased out by a night security guard. Chris and I spent the night and headed back up to Fort Collins in the morning. In the end, my friend had some complicated things going on in life, so a romantic relationship wasn't possible.

We remained close friends and kept in touch over the years. There were times we'd lose contact for a stretch, but somehow we'd always reconnect. At one point when I was a junior in college, we thought we had another chance, but this time some of my life circumstances and our distance made it impossible. She had moved to Hawaii with her family, so even if I had a car, it wouldn't have done me any good. I would have needed a boat, or at least the money for a plane ticket. Obviously God had different plans for both of us. In one of her letters to me, she ventured that we had gotten it right in another life. We're now both married with families of our own and are still friends some twenty years after those three days at camp and one of the most crazy road trips I've ever taken.

For the record, my first car was a late-eighties Oldsmobile Cutlass I bought from my dad for one thousand dollars when I was twenty-four. I got a lot of good use out of it, but that car's life ended after dodging one bullet but getting obliterated by another.

One night in 2000, I was awakened by the sound of someone pounding on my apartment door. Half asleep and rubbing my eyes, I opened the door and it was the fire department. "Sir, we need you to get out of your apartment right away and go across the street!" I didn't need to ask what was going on. Behind him, the entire apartment parking structure and dozens of cars were ablaze. The smell of burning rubber and metal filled the air and huge flames shot up and licked the night sky. I was directed across the street and stood there in disbelief with my fellow apartment residents as we watched the flames move from one car to the next. It was ruled as arson, but the police never caught anyone. Although I felt bad for everyone who lost a car, I was secretly relieved that I had decided to park on the street that evening after work, and so my car was spared the carnage. In fact, I counted myself rather lucky. But how lucky can one man get? A week later as I slowed to stop at an intersection on the way home from work, a Salvation Army donation truck driver who thought I would try to beat the red, sped up and rear-ended me. The impact shot me across the intersection, and it took me several seconds to even realize what had happened. Luckily I was unhurt, but my car was totaled, and with it, any notion that some divine intervention had spared my car the night of the fire. I spent the next several months battling the Salvation Army's insurance company and finally got a check for the resale value of my car, which wasn't much. It was, however, a partial down payment on my next car, a blue Dodge Neon. Regardless, it's not that a car would have impressed my friend when I showed up for her birthday–far from it. I could tell when we met that she had a kind of hippy nature and didn't care too much about material things. Still, the trip down in a car would've been a lot more comfortable and offered far fewer brushes with death. On the other hand, it wouldn't have provided such a memorable story, or the turning point for a life-long friendship.

# THE CROWD YOU FIT
# IN WITH MAY NOT BE
# WHAT YOU EXPECT

*An identity would seem to be arrived at by the way in
which the person faces and uses his experience.*
*—James Baldwin*

E veryone who leaves home for college faces a time of transition.
It's a time of newly- discovered freedom away from parents and a
place to become your true self. After I started school at Colorado
State University, I went out to find my place on campus. I was hardly
the coolest person in my dorm, but compared to the guy who walked
around our hall in nothing but briefs and a toy Star Trek phaser clipped
to the elastic, I was socially well adjusted. I didn't really fit in squarely
or exclusively with any particular group on my dorm floor. I had
friends who were former high school athletes, friends who were strict
Christians, and others who smoked pot and drank beer every day. Part
of this was because of my compulsion to get along with everyone I'm
around, and part of it was because I hadn't yet really defined who I am
as an individual.

Like many other Asian Americans, I checked out my school's Asian/
Pacific- American Student Services (APASS). I didn't know what to
expect the night I decided to attend my first APASS meeting, but let's
just say it was the first—and last—one I ever attended. I walked across
campus thinking this would be a good opportunity for me to meet some
people I could fit in with. I nervously entered the room where everyone
was gathered and figured someone would probably greet me, or at least

acknowledge my presence. Something like "Hi, I haven't seen you here before, is this your first meeting?" Again, I admit I'm relatively shy in new crowds, but that night, I felt like a fly on the wall—completely invisible through the entire meeting.

A mix of one-and-a-half generation Asian Americans and international students made up a majority of the crowd. Most of them grew up with Asian parents and had last names like Park, Chang, and Tanaka. They chatted away in their native languages, and I felt more and more like an outsider. It was one of the most uncomfortable settings I've ever been in. That night, I had set out to search for companionship with "my own" but instead, I left just feeling alienated.

I really only had one or two Asian friends during college, but these relationships came about more by chance than design or a conscious effort on my part. The summer between my sophomore and junior year, I rented out a room in a fraternity house and met a Japanese exchange student who became a good pal. However, it was our penchant for goofing off and getting into trouble that made us close—not being Asian. In fact, I got grossed out every time he would broil a whole fish and use chopsticks to pick the entire thing clean—including the head.

When I look back, I can't help but think that perhaps my experience with the APASS group was just because I don't have an outgoing personality and am rather shy in new situations. Maybe I should've given it a second shot, but years later, I discovered I wasn't completely alone.

During graduate school at New York University, my thesis advisor and I were talking about adoption and culture. He recalled a story similar to mine about his friend's daughter, who was also adopted from Korea. She had a similar experience when she attended her school's Asian Student Association meeting for the first time. Nothing the group did or talked about was relevant to her, and like me, she felt marginalized and never went back. Two people hardly represent the entire adopted community, but it did make me think. For us, merely being Asian wasn't enough to benefit from joining an Asian Student Association.

When I moved to the Bay Area after college, I knew I'd be around a lot more Asians, and again for some reason thought this would also somehow benefit me. I enjoyed many days and nights exploring San Francisco's Chinatown and Japantown, but just like in college, I ended up just fitting in with whomever I was around. The majority of the people where I lived in Oakland were African American, and just like in college, I got along with pretty much everyone.

I've learned over time that without shared experiences and needs, the simple fact that you look like other people in a group doesn't guarantee a personal bond. The night at my university's APASS meeting and for three years in California, other Asians and I may have been birds of a racial "feather," but I was definitely not part of the flock.

# CHERISH TIME WITH
## YOUR SIBLINGS: IT'S LIMITED

*Other things may change us, but*
*we start and end with the family.*
—*Anthony Brandt*

Death is a part of life. Most of us at some point will lose a parent or grandparent, aunt or uncle. However, nothing ever really prepares you to lose a child or sibling at a young age. Two days after Thanksgiving in 1999, my dad called me in Walnut Creek, California from Denver and left a voicemail asking me to return his call as soon as possible. I quickly dialed home, and when my dad answered, his voice was subdued. I could tell right away that something was wrong.

"I'm afraid we have some terrible news," he said preparing me for what was to come. When someone leads with that, you can at least try to prepare yourself mentally. "Your brother took his own life last night." I wasn't prepared for that. At that instant, time froze. I was in total shock and disbelief. Our entire conversation seemed like a surreal dream. After we hung up, I sat stunned and unable to move or think. It took me some time before I could stand up and get my thoughts together.

This wasn't the first time I'd dealt with a suicide—and it wouldn't be the last. A few months after I moved to California, I found out one of my friends that I lived with in Colorado had hanged himself. Years later, after I moved back to Colorado, I was the unfortunate one to find a friend and co-worker at his home after he didn't show up for work. I went to his house to check on him. His truck was in the driveway and the front door was unlocked. After calling his name and searching the house, I eventually discovered him in the basement, dead after shooting himself. The tragic nature of a friend's suicide will shake any person up, but it's especially devastating when it's a family member.

My brother Nicholas was home from college for the Thanksgiving holiday, and according to our parents, everything seemed normal. He went shopping with our dad the day after Thanksgiving and showed no outward signs of trouble or depression. That night in his room, he overdosed on sleeping pills and never woke up. Since that day, November has been bittersweet for my family. It's a time of thanksgiving and heartbreak and loss as we pause each year to remember Nick.

My brother was an amazing young man. He was a dreamer and a visionary. He was an idealist driven by a fervent faith in God and others. He was an artist and philosopher whose love of music was both infectious and inspirational. He was an individual whose spirit drew people close to him.

*Jenn and Nick enjoying our tire swing together*

Nick was born in 1980 in Calcutta, India, and originally named Anil. He contracted polio as an infant and spent the first two years of his life in one of Mother Teresa's orphanages before my parents adopted him into our family. Without the use of his legs, he got around with a walker, crutches, and later, a wheelchair. A disability that might lead a person of lesser resolve to a mediocre or bitter existence instead inspired my brother to live his life to the fullest.

I remember the day when we met and brought Nick home from the airport on his adoption day. Being two years old, he had already picked up some basic Hindi words and even a little song he would sing over and over. Like most toddlers, Nick was curious, full of life, and became attached to a few particular toys.

Nick and I always shared a room growing up, and I have fond memories of our late nights talking and giggling and goofing off. We slept in bunk beds, and our favorite game was "fishing." With our combined imaginations, we transformed my top bunk into a fishing boat, and his lower bunk into the ocean. I would lower down my sheet, which was the fishing line, and Nick would tug on it and tell me what I had caught. At one point, my mom had to un-bunk our beds and move us to separate sides of our room. "Cut the clowning around. If I have to come in here one more time, you're not going to like the consequences," she'd warn us night after night. We didn't let that stop us, and we tossed stuffed animals back and forth from bed to bed, snickering as quietly as possible.

From a young age, Nick never let his condition slow him down. He skied with a special mono-ski, rode horses, played wheelchair basketball, and was even in his high school's marching band. Growing up, his interest in music began to blossom. He played the flute, guitar, and later became an avid drummer. One of our family's favorite memories is how one summer Nick secretly purchased a drum set piece by piece from a local music shop and hid it under his bed.

*Nick playing drums in his dorm room*

Nick was a sophomore at Colorado State University, the same school I attended. Still a teenager, he had his whole life and a promising future ahead of him. To this day, none of us fully understand why he took his own life. The real reasons are something that those who loved him will never grasp. Even though I regret not calling him more often at school, all I can do is cherish the memories of growing up together and give thanks for the time I got to spend with him.

He sent a final email to family and friends and tried to explain why he left us. At times, I still find myself pulling out the email I printed out and tucked into a shoebox many years ago. This was before smart phones, and I hadn't checked my email before my dad called that day. At the end of the letter, Nick pasted in the lyrics from the song "Naked" by The Goo Goo Dolls to summarize how he felt.

Nick's impact on people's lives was evident in the days and weeks after his death. At a memorial for him at the university, friends and faculty packed into the room to remember my brother. Nick had taken the job of checking student IDs at the entrance to the dining hall and had come to know and befriend just about everyone in his dorm. He had also taken his drum set up to school and became notorious on his floor for breaking quiet hours but also famous for his self-taught percussion skills and love of music. His dorm RA would often visit Nick's room after quiet hours to tell him to knock it off.

I learned this little fact as part of a pretty cool coincidence. I had briefly met Noah, Nick's dorm RA at the memorial service at the university. Years later at the Korean Heritage Camp, we crossed paths again, but it took us a while to piece together where we had seen each other before. Noah and I finally realized the connection and went on to become good friends. It was first in a string of almost surreal similarities in our lives. We were both Korean adoptees and both received our degree in graphic design from Colorado State University. There were many other weird parallels with our families and personal lives. We even found out that both of our cars had been rear ended at the exact same intersection. Of course, the most important connection was that Nick had been a part of both of our lives.

*Special needs* is a term commonly used to refer to children with a mental or physical disability, and the adoption process usually moves faster for a family willing to adopt a special needs child. The more I think about this term, the more I dislike it. Not because it's politically incorrect, but because it's misleading. *All* children have special needs. Some children are clingy and others are independent. One might need a night light to sleep and another might need extra tutoring in math. Nick was a kid who overcame adversity and achieved great things. For this, I don't view him as having been someone with special needs in the traditional sense of the word; he was just someone who was simply special.

# LOVE CAN REALLY MAKE YOU SICK

*I was nauseous and tingly all over...*
*I was either in love or I had smallpox.*
*—Woody Allen*

Any time I fill out a form at a doctor's office, or a nurse asks me about my family's health history, I answer one way: "I don't know. I'm adopted." This fact also got me out of an entire high school biology exercise to track our dominant and recessive traits based on our physical features. While it's possible for me to control my lifestyle, family background is still an important indicator of risk for certain health conditions.

I do what I can to stay healthy. I don't drink excessively or smoke, and I try to eat a balanced diet. When I lived in Colorado, I took advantage of the outdoors and became an avid runner, rock climber, hiker, and mountain biker. I trained and ran a couple of half-marathons, and in 2003, I completed my first full one. After moving to New York, my active life slowed down quite a bit, but I still try to get as much exercise as my schedule and environment allow. These things alone make me confident I can live a relatively disease-free life, but the fact I don't know if there's a history of cancer or strokes in my biological family does unnerve me sometimes.

So far, the two semiserious health problems I've dealt with are diverticulitis, which is a small area in the intestine that becomes infected and painfully inflamed, and back problems caused by flat feet. When the first condition flared up and left me incapacitated, I was scheduled to fly to New York and ask my father-in-law for permission to marry Becky. Becky and I met and fell in love through an unlikely series of events. Here's our back-story.

Becky was born in Seoul, and in 1977 when she was two years old, her parents took her and her younger sister and moved to South America. They lived briefly in Paraguay and Argentina before settling in Caracas, Venezuela where Becky's younger brother Peter was born in 1980. Times were tough though, and between 1981 and 1982, Becky and her siblings went to live with her grandparents in Mankato, Minnesota. Amazingly, this is just thirty miles from New Ulm, where my mom was born and raised. However, my family had already moved from Minneapolis, so Becky and I missed being in the same state by a couple of years. In 1986, Becky's whole family was reunited in Queens, New York. In 1990, Becky moved by herself back to Minnesota and lived with her grandparents for a year before returning to New York where she and her family have lived since.

In 2003, I was in Denver working on my MBA. Becky's membership to a site called Christian Cafe was going to expire at the end of the year, so she called to cancel it. Meanwhile, I'd gone through a couple of bad relationships, and a friend of mine half-jokingly suggested that I try to meet someone online. I figured I didn't have anything to lose, so I joined Christian Cafe in December and started to see who was out there.

I noticed from Becky's profile that she is Korean-American, and on January 2, 2004, I sent her an e-mail just to say hi. Not realizing she was about to meet her future husband, Becky called Christian Cafe to complain because they automatically renewed her membership—despite her earlier cancellation. A little while later, she received my message in her Christian Cafe inbox and decided to write back. We started to chat on the phone, and sometime later, we decided to meet.

In May 2004 after final exams, I flew out to New York for the first time and got to know Becky in person. Call both of us crazy, but by the end of the week, we knew we were supposed to spend the rest of our lives together.

Because of my classes, Becky's schedule was more flexible than mine, and she flew out to Denver as much as possible over the next year. Because she couldn't leave her family business, I decided to quit my job at the bank where I worked and move to New York. That November, I proposed.

We had talked about marriage, but Becky had no idea I was going to propose during her visit after Thanksgiving. By all accounts, the actual proposal was a mess. I tripped over my words and put the ring on the wrong hand, but she still said yes. She also told me that I needed to go to New York and ask her dad in person for permission to marry her. I had previously met Becky's dad when I visited her the first time, but having to get his formal blessing did stress me out. However, I loved Becky and was willing to do it for her.

I was scheduled to fly to New York in December before Christmas, and after the New Year, Becky planned to come to Denver so we could drive back to New York together. The morning of my flight, I woke up with a sharp pain in my abdomen. In typical male fashion, I thought maybe I could tough it out, so I called Becky. "Hi, honey. I woke up with a bad pain in my lower abdomen, but I think I can make my flight if I try," I rationalized though gritted teeth.

"Are you crazy?" she exclaimed in disbelief. "Go to the emergency room now! Your appendix may have burst or something."

"Okay, I just don't want to disappoint your dad," I apologized. Getting sick at exactly this time sounded like the kind of lame excuse for cold feet that someone writes into a sitcom plot.

I hung up the phone and rushed to the emergency clinic. By the time I arrived, I was feverish, nauseated, and constipated. The nurse hooked me up to an IV for a couple of hours and sent me home with a laxative, instructions for an all-liquid diet, and an appointment for a colonoscopy. I went home to prepare for my procedure, and anyone who's had a colonoscopy knows how unpleasant it is. Luckily for me, Becky was on her way to Denver for our drive back to New York.

After the procedure, I came out of general anesthesia groggy and dazed, and Becky guided me out of the hospital and into my car. We had a few days before I had to vacate my apartment, so I got to rest, but this is basically how we started our new life together. To this day, Becky is convinced that the stress from me having to ask her dad for permission to marry her played a big part in the whole thing.

The second health issue, which also left me incapacitated for a couple of days, was when my lower back went out due to problems that stemmed from my flat feet. It had happened a couple times before, but the most recent was in 2006 at a church picnic. I was playing soccer when a sharp pain suddenly hit my lower back like an electric shock. It was the kind of pain that made it nearly impossible to walk, bend over, or even sit down. Nevertheless, as a man, I planned to just suck it up. Becky had different ideas. "You're going to the acupuncturist," she insisted as we drove back to Flushing. Incidentally, my brother-in-law sprained his ankle in the same soccer game, so both of us had to go.

"Are you serious?" I questioned Becky and flashed a skeptical look her way.

"Well, it's Sunday, and no doctor is available, so unless you want to suffer all night, this is the only option," she advised.

This concept was something completely foreign to me. As someone who was always treated with Western medicine, I equated acupuncture with quackery and on par with being bled by leeches. However, the pain got worse, and eventually I would have accepted voodoo if it gave me some relief. So, both my ego and I limped into the acupuncturist office and, just like during my colonoscopy, I found myself half-naked and facedown on an examination table. However, this time the doctor was a Korean man with a container full of needles and I was fully conscious.

After strategically sticking multiple needles all over my body, the acupuncturist started placing some small objects on my back. I heard the unmistakable sound of a match striking, and this made me even more nervous. After a minute or so, I felt a hot, almost burning sensation on my back and started to smell smoke. Afterward, Becky told me they were small jars filled with incense and attached to the skin in a technique called *boo woong.* "Just relax," the acupuncturist said.

*Yeah, I always relax when I have little things burning on my back,* I thought to myself.

I don't know if the ritual actually did anything medically, but at least for a moment, the intense heat took my mind off the original pain in my back.

The next day, as Becky helped me out of bed, she kissed me and warned, "You're my husband, and I love you, but if our children have flat feet, I'm going to kill you!" Our son Jeremy inherited many of my features, but Becky is so amused by the fact his feet are exact little carbon copies of mine that she decided to give me a pass.

# If You're Going to Rebel, at Least Do It Right

*Good tattoos aren't cheap, and cheap tattoos aren't good.*
*—Unknown*

Most of us have done something earlier in life that we wouldn't do over if given a choice. The consequences of many of our regretful actions are fleeting—others are more permanent. Listening to heavy metal was one of my forms of rebellion. My parents hated it, but I loved it. The first time I heard Metallica in 6th grade, I was hooked. Keeping in line with the culture, I wanted to get my ear pierced, but my parents wouldn't allow it when I was still living at home. Growing my hair long and sporting a denim jacket with back patches and buttons of my favorite bands was as far as they allowed me to go. "You're not allowed to get your ear pierced as long as you're living under our roof," they said.

"Well, I'll just do it after I move out then," I said defiantly. So, when I got to college, I got my ear pierced within the first week. During the next four years, I ended up also getting a couple of tattoos: a yin-yang on my shoulder and "the eyes of Bodhnath," or Buddha's eyes, on my chest. Like many others who get tattoos in their youth, I did so without much foresight. At that point, I was still trying to discover who I was and thought these permanent additions to my body would be a good way to embrace and display my Eastern roots. This was long before I became a Christian again after first leaving home, and I now prefer to keep my tattoos covered at all times. In fact, a lot of people close to me don't even know I have them.

The first month I moved to New York, a huge blizzard swept in
and buried the city under a blanket of white. Becky's dad had a snow
blower in his garage, and he needed to get it out and take it to the
family business. There was just one problem, though: The garage door
was stuck, and we had to open it from the inside.

Becky's dad approaches all projects—big or small—with a thorough
explanation and detailed plan of attack. He sat down at the kitchen table
with a pen and pad of paper and called me to join him. Speaking enough
English to communicate, he started to sketch a diagram of what we needed
to do. "First, we take out garage door window, and someone go inside to
open the door," he explained as a crude diagram of the garage took shape on
the pad. I struggled to make sense of it, but perhaps as a former art student
and Pictionary aficionado, I was being too critical. "Before, I was very thin,
so I could fit, but now I'm too old and big. You understand?" he asked.

He then illustrated how the rod mechanism worked on the door and
told me how it was stuck. I simply nodded in agreement. The entire
explanation took a good twenty minutes, and just as he was almost done,
Steve, Becky's sister's husband, showed up. Unable to have someone who
didn't know the whole story join the operation, Becky's dad told Steve to
sit down, and he started the whole explanation over from the start.

We finally decided that we'd remove the windowpane and then boost
Steve up so he could squeeze through the opening. Once the door was
open, we'd cover the window with cardboard and duct tape until we
could replace it.

The plan went into action, and we pulled it off flawlessly. So after
our little chore, Becky's dad told us we were just "going to lunch." He
said something in Korean, and Steve got kind of nervous; I could tell he
knew something I didn't. Neither of us had a choice though, so we got
in the car and went along with whatever was in store.

Becky's dad pulled into the parking lot of a business that had a sign
in Korean, and in English, it displayed only the word *Sauna*. I had never
heard of a *Jjimjilbang* (Korean public bathhouse), let alone gone to one;
however, that was about to change. The three of us went inside, Becky's
dad checked us in at the front desk, and he handed both Steve and me

a locker key. Once in the locker room, I honestly had no idea what was going on, but before I knew it, Becky's dad stripped down right in front of us and simply walked into the sauna area and left us standing there.

After a moment of awkward silence passed, Steve finally spoke up. "Uh, I guess we should go in." *Oh, crap*, I thought to myself. *My future father-in-law is going to see my tattoos!* There was nothing I could do at that point short of running out and going home to hide, so I reluctantly shed my clothes and entered the sauna area buck naked, as a wall of humid air enveloped my body. The main area featured a large Roman-style hot soaking pool, and there were hot steam rooms and showers all around the perimeter. These saunas are rooted in the tradition of public bathhouses in Korea that became popular in the early part of the twentieth century before most homes had modern bathrooms.

Steve and I quickly slipped into the hot pool trying to avoid eye contact, and the three of us soaked in uncomfortable silence. It was one of many moments when I was glad I didn't speak Korean. I knew of course that Becky's dad could see my tattoos. There was no hiding–well–anything. But if he couldn't ask, I didn't have to tell.

After our sauna session, we ate lunch and headed back to the family business with the snowplow. We arrived home refreshed with rosy glows on our faces and toothpicks dangling out of our mouths. Becky and her sister were waiting, irate at our long delay. "Where the heck have you been?" Becky demanded as her dad explained in Korean and smoothed everything out the best he could. Later that night, I was chatting with Becky about how weird the sauna experience was. "Did your dad say anything about my tattoos?" I asked tentatively.

"Yeah. He didn't care," she replied. I felt good until she continued, "The only thing he said is that he was unimpressed, and if he wanted to get a tattoo, at least he could have gotten something really big and fancy like a cool dragon or something."

I didn't know whether to be relieved that they didn't bother him or insulted that he didn't think they were good enough. All in all, it wasn't easy accepting the premise that I hadn't even rebelled correctly, so it's a good thing I had taken my earrings out years before.

# BE HONORED WHEN SOMEONE
## TAKES YOUR NAME

*Better to see the face than to hear the name.*
*—Unknown*

Growing up in America, I didn't think much about the name my adoptive parents gave me. I was Peter for as far back as I can remember, so it was never strange to me. The only time I mentioned my Korean moniker was when someone asked if I knew it. "Kim, Jai Chul," I'd reply proudly, as if I'd just nailed a Final Jeopardy question with my entire winnings on the line.

It wasn't until I married a Lee did I fully understand the importance that many Koreans place on family names. Seriously, is there a Korean Lee in existence who can't trace their ancestors directly to aristocracy of the Joseon Dynasty? Joseon was Korea's last and longest running Confucian dynasty and laid the foundation for much of the nation's modern culture.

I feel lucky that Becky traded the Lee name for Moran. Becky's sister and most of our Korean friends kept their last names. In fact, traditionally in Korea, wives never took their husband's family name. Other reasons our friends gave for not changing included career identity and the difficult process to replace their driver's license and bankcards. My mother-in-law wasn't entirely convinced about Becky's name change either. "Mo-ran, Mo-ran, what kind of name is that?" she yelled in half-joking disapproval. "My daughter's new name sounds like moron!" Moron. Like I hadn't heard that before. But to be fair, it would be difficult for Rockefeller or Kennedy to pass the initial scrutiny of a traditional Korean mother. Likewise, Becky's dad had a hard time accepting the fact his oldest daughter was no longer a Lee, and a couple of years went by after Becky and I got married before he finally began to introduce her to strangers as Becky Moran.

Adoptive families and adoptees deal with names differently. My parents assigned my adopted siblings' names to their middle names, and some parents who adopted older children let them choose their own names. One friend of mine found the most personal identity and pride in his Korean name and decided to legally change his last name back to Kim. "I got tired of telling strangers why I have a German last name and don't want my children to go through the same thing," he explained unapologetically.

Although I didn't think about my adoption all the time, I still had the same questions and uncertainties a lot of adoptees have. Who are my birth parents, and where are they now? Do I have any biological brothers or sisters? I'm sure such questions vary for a child who was adopted at an older age instead of as a baby, but there is a common thread to both experiences. It's something that moves us all, whether we're adopted or not—a desire to know our origins and an unspoken bond between flesh and blood that transcends cultures and continents.

As a teenager, I told my mom I never wanted to get married or have kids. I'm not sure exactly why I had made up my mind so early. Now a husband and father, I can't imagine life any other way. Becky and I tried for several years to start a family. Our first pregnancy miscarried after eight weeks. Our second pregnancy started as triplets, and as we shared the news, our friends and family reacted with shock and joy. I'll never forget my father-in-law's initial response. "It's three babies," I beamed with pride. He didn't get it at first, but after several attempts to explain it, he finally realized what I was saying. "Becky always has to overdo everything," he replied in his typical critical but loving fashion.

As the pregnancy progressed, our joy and excitement was tempered, as only one of the embryos became viable. Becky carried Elijah for almost six months, but we lost him to pre-term labor. The doctors told us it was a blood clot, which caused the placenta to detach from Elijah and then forced Becky into labor. It was a bitter pill to swallow, but we tried again and got pregnant with twins. Again, Becky carried them through five months, but we also lost Luke and Isabelle to pre-term labor complications.

Luke's water broke prematurely, and the risk to Isabelle and Becky were too high to continue. At first, we thought we had a choice. "If you decide to continue, the boy will face great odds without any amniotic fluid," the doctor explained. "At this point in the pregnancy, this fluid is critical to the baby's final development." Becky and I discussed it and decided that we wanted to continue with the pregnancy. No matter what the odds, we would do everything we could.

Our hope withered away though, as other doctors got involved and decided there was no choice. An infection had now made its way into the womb, and they told us that the first priority was Becky's health. If we didn't terminate the pregnancy, the infection could progress beyond the stage of antibiotics. We didn't get to see Luke after he was delivered, but the doctors did allow us to hold and spend as much time as we needed to with Isabelle after her birth and immediate passing.

Afterward, one of the doctors sat down and talked with us. "Doctors have been delivering babies for thousands of years and a lot of it is still a mystery to us," he explained.

Watching our first three babies come into the world but not get to take them home was the worst thing that either of us had experienced and endured. All three of them are buried close to one another in Long Island. Heartbroken, we tried again, and the pregnancy started with twins. However, only one embryo

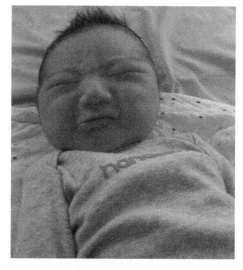

*Jeremy showing attitude at two-days-old*

*Jeremy's tummy time with Dad*

became viable. This time, we kept the news of Becky's pregnancy quiet. It felt like an eternity waiting for the 24-week mark—the time period after which a baby can make it outside of the womb. First six months passed, then seven and eight. Although a few weeks early, on June 13, 2011, God blessed us with a beautiful baby boy.

After everything we'd been through, the last thing Becky wanted was a baby shower. In fact, she specifically instructed her sister Sunny not to throw one. We had learned over the years not to take anything for granted and for us, a baby shower seemed like a premature celebration. However, after seven months into the pregnancy, Sunny informed me she was planning a surprise shower anyway. Although I was in on the surprise, there was an extra twist to the plan that even I didn't know about—something that would catch me completely off guard.

It was a Saturday, and I knew I had to get up and help set up the yard for the shower. I had just woken up and was still in my pajamas when Sunny called me downstairs for some fake reason I can't even remember anymore. I headed down the staircase, as we're on the second floor of a two-family home we live in with Sunny and Steve. Sunny opened the door to their home, and I did a double take at the person standing there. "Uh, hi Mom...what are you doing here?" I said still half asleep and unable to put two and two together. Sunny had secretly flown my mom out from Colorado to attend the shower and there I stood—speechless in my pajamas with everyone laughing at my puzzled look. I have to admit, I never saw it coming, but my little surprise was a prelude of what was to come. The day's plot still had a lot of thickening.

Becky's family business has an office in Queens and one in New Jersey. At the time, Sunny was managing the New Jersey store. The day of the shower, Sunny never showed up to work because she was running around preparing for the party. Naturally, Becky kept trying to get hold of Sunny on her cell phone, but Sunny wasn't answering–and it was all of our jobs to cover for her. It wasn't long before my phone started ringing. "Hey have you seen Sunny?" Becky inquired.

"No, why, what's going on?" I asked feigning ignorance.

"She never showed up to work, and she's not answering her phone."

"Hmm...yeah, she's not here. I don't know, I'll ask Steve if he knows."

"Anyway, if you hear from her, tell her to call me 'cause I'm really getting pissed off."

"Okay," I said, trying to sound as sincerely concerned as possible. It's never a good thing to lie to your wife, but sometimes you just have to do what you have to do. Besides, I wasn't going to be a party pooper.

By the afternoon, Becky was fuming. Apparently, she had briefly gotten hold of Sunny who told her she'd been in a car accident but couldn't talk because her phone was about to die. This tall tale of course made Becky even more worried, and she was waiting at the Queens office for Sunny to show up there–which of course never happened. My phone rang again.

"Is Sunny home?" Becky asked, obviously very irritated.

"No," I continued the charade.

"Maybe you should just come home, honey," I suggested after she had called a few more times. It was now my duty to get Becky to come home. All the guests had arrived, the food was prepared, and we were ready to start. We knew no matter how mad Becky was, the second she saw what was going on, all would be forgiven.

What seemed like hours later, I finally saw Becky's car turn the corner onto our block. "She's coming!" I yelled, signaling everyone to get ready for the big surprise–not like there was a place for everyone to hide. Becky inched closer and finally turned into the driveway, which was full of family and friends. Through the windshield, I saw her furious face change to one of surprise and then melt into tears. For a second, Becky thought it was a dream, and like me, it took her a while to process that my mom was standing there in a crowd of other family and friends. It was a wonderful party, and Becky did end up forgiving Sunny for everything that had happened beforehand. We spent the next several weeks waiting in anticipation for our son to enter the world.

Like many parents, we struggled to decide on a name. It was easy for Elijah, Luke and Isabelle—it's hard to argue when you're grieving and in shock. We picked their names right at the hospital. "How about Luke?" I had suggested, thinking both of the Biblical name and my favorite movie, *Star Wars*. I'm not sure where the name Isabelle came from. I just remember is sounded nice. It was different for Jeremy. We wanted a name nobody else had in our extended families. We scoured through the baby name books, arguing and debating over this and that name. It's common for second-generation Korean-Americans to give their children a Judeo-Christian first name and a Korean middle name, and we finally decided on Jeremy Sejong. The name Jeremy is Hebrew for "God will raise up." We named him Sejong after Sejong the Great, the king who created the Korean alphabet. *Se* means "world," and *jong* is "the top of a hill." We picked Sejong because some friends of ours commented that I bore a striking resemblance to the fifteenth-century Korean king. We Googled King Sejong and were amazed and amused at how similar we look.

Even though Jeremy isn't adopted and has two Korean parents, he'll still go through life as a Korean with an Irish last name. He and his kids will still have to explain when people comment that he doesn't look like a Moran. I looked up the origin of the name Moran and found it's derived from the Gaelic Ó Móráin, which means "descendant of the great one." I don't really subscribe to pop psychology, but if it's true that a person's name can influence his or her personality, there's no way our son can fail.

# VISITING THE COUNTRY OF YOUR ANCESTORS IS A BUCKET LIST MUST

*I came to the place of my birth and cried,*
*The friends of my youth, where are they?*
*An echo answered, Where are they?*
*—Arabic Proverb*

*Changgyeonggung Palace: built by King Sejong*
*in 1418 for his father, former King Taejong*

Whether you're adopted or not, there's just something special about exploring your roots and the land you came from. In March 2008, I got this opportunity and took my first "real" trip back to Korea. I say "real" because I had been in the Seoul airport a couple of times as a connection point to and from Thailand for church mission trips in 2006 and 2007. I never counted this, though, because I didn't get to step outside of the airport. Sure, I was technically in Korea, but the international terminal didn't provide the full experience I was looking for.

Our journey to Korea was the apex of my adoption story. It was both the end point to a lifetime of wonderment and the genesis to an entire new line of questions. I consider myself lucky that I not only got to visit my motherland, but I got to share the journey with my wife. Becky had been to Korea several times before, so she acted as tour guide and translator. It was extra nice because Becky and I stopped off in Hawaii for a few days and got to enjoy the warmth before Korea, which in March was still snowy and bone-chilling cold. We also got the chance to visit some of her dad's family.

I had talked for years about taking a trip to Korea. Most of the time it was just casual like, *Yeah, I'll make it one day before I die.* When I was a teenager, my parents told me that they gave their full support should I ever want to conduct a birth parent search. They prepared me for the odds of finding anything, but even in the 90s, many of the resources available today in Korea just didn't exist. Today, there are Korean television programs that feature videos of adoptees telling their stories in hopes that their birth parents will see them. We didn't stay in Korea long enough to do one of these videos, but we still found something.

While soul-searching, Becky and I visited several organizations and followed a trail of breadcrumbs that lead us to the children's hospital where I briefly stayed as a newborn. We started at GOA'L (Global Overseas Adoptees' Link) headquarters. We met with the president of the organization, and after we explained my story, he made a call to Holt Children's Services Post Adoption Service Center and set up a meeting for us with a Holt social worker. We stayed and chatted a while longer and then headed out to the next stop in our hunt for answers.

When we arrived at Holt Children's Services, a social worker named Seol, Eun greeted and handed us her business card. Becky explained we were the couple that GOA'L had called about. The social worker went

to an old metal file cabinet and pulled
out my file, which was no more than a
few sheets of paper in a yellow manila
folder. At first, she indicated that there
really wasn't any information she
could give. Believing we had reached
the end of the road, Becky and I were
disappointed and got ready to leave.
Before we got up, the social worker
suggested that Becky and I visit the
children's hospital. She mentioned
it almost as an afterthought, but I'm
glad she did. The hospital is where I
eventually found my record and birth
mother's name.

*The hospital where I found my birth record*

The hospital is located on the
outskirts of Seoul, and the social worker told us the only way to get there
was by taxi, as the subway didn't go that far out of the main part of the
city. It wasn't easy getting to the hospital but once we arrived, a volunteer
social worker met with us and helped locate my adoption record.

After Becky explained my story in Korean, the social worker led us
to a room, which was more of a storage closet full of old record books,
all of which they hadn't transferred to computers yet. Using my name
and birth date, she located a book, brushed off the dust, and carefully
leafed through the pages. Becky and I held our breath in anticipation,
and after what felt like an eternity, the social worker found my
record. It noted my birth mother's name as Kang, Hee Sook (in Korea,
surnames are written first, so her family name is Kang and her first
name Hee Sook). The record also gave a brief description of why she
left me, but there was no additional information such as a national ID
number (similar to a U.S. social security number) that provided an easy
way to track her down.

The social worker explained in Korean while Becky translated. "Korea
was still a poor country when you were born."

She then offered me her personal apology on behalf of the country for giving me up. "I'm sorry that we couldn't take care of you." I'm happy with my life and didn't need an explanation or apology, but her touching gesture moved Becky and me to tears.

As we both fought back our emotions, the social worker then told us that Hee Sook didn't actually name me. She explained that when I was born, hospitals commonly gave all abandoned children the hospital administrator's family name for ease and expediency. In May 1975, that name happened to be Kim. I don't know my birth father's family name, and in all probability never will, but I'm happy with Kim. Sure, it's not Lee, but it's still *yang-ban* (noble).

Becky and I plan to go back to Korea again some day with Jeremy and do an additional search for my birth mother. Perhaps my hope to track her down and meet in person is a pipe dream, but for me, the adventure and discovery along the way was inherently fulfilling the first time, and I'm sure it will be again.

# BEING AN AMERICAN ABROAD HAS ITS UPS AND DOWNS

*There are no foreign lands. It is the
traveler only who is foreign.*
—Robert Louis Stevenson

*Affectionate pachyderms during a 2006 Thailand mission trip*

The trips outside of the United States I've been fortunate enough
to take include camping in Canada, Thailand for two church
mission trips, Aruba for our honeymoon, and the trip Becky and
I took to Korea. In all instances, including Korea, the locals were able

to instantly identify us as Americans. In Aruba, I of course expected it. From the "independent" cabdriver that gave us a ride to the hotel from the airport, to the "land sharks" a.k.a. timeshare salespeople, they all pegged us as obvious tourists the second we stepped off the plane.

When Becky and I went to Korea, for some reason, I believed we'd be able to blend in; after all, we look like everyone else there. Nope. Again, people recognized us as Americans right off the plane. However, for a brief moment, this was actually a positive thing. It turned out my hair (or lack of it) created a case of mistaken identity and almost got us VIP treatment.

In 2006, I started shaving my head. From the time I first noticed my hairline thinning, I decided it was all coming off—no Rogaine or holding desperately to the scraps, just a nice clean break and the easiest boot camp-style haircut in the world. Plus, since I shave my own head, we've saved hundreds in haircuts over the years.

Moments after we stepped off the plane into the Seoul Incheon International Airport terminal, a greeter for US military personnel and their spouses automatically approached and ushered us toward an area for special transportation accommodations. "Right this way, sir," the man gestured, speaking in English. Confused, Becky and I looked at each other and began to follow him with hesitation. He turned and saw we were not entirely sure what was going on. "You're an American GI, right?" he asked tentatively after realizing the potential error of his assumption.

"No, I'm not in the military," I replied.

"Oh, sorry. I thought you were a soldier," he said while pointing to my shaved head. In the end, we took the regular bus from the airport into Seoul, which is about a forty-five-minute ride. The windy snow-dusted landscape between Incheon Airport and Seoul was a drastic change from the warm beaches of Waikiki we were laying on days earlier.

We stayed with friends who are originally from Los Angeles but had moved to Korea for work. After adjusting to the time change as much as possible, we ventured out to explore the city on our own during the week. Aside from the airport incident, I experienced a few other unexpected twists during the first trip back to my birth country.

The first day, our friends left for work, and Becky and I got ready to head out. I was about to get in the shower, and even though I was previously in the bathroom, I suddenly realized there was no shower curtain. Perplexed but not wanting to ask Becky to call our friends and ask if they had a shower curtain, I turned the shower head as far to the inside as it would go and tried to keep water from going out. Despite my best efforts, by the end of my shower, I had created a lake on the toilet and floor. I took a towel and mopped up the mess the best I could. "Honey, you know there isn't a shower curtain?" I asked as I emerged from the bathroom, being careful not to slip on the remaining puddles. "I don't understand what happened. Water got all over the place," I said, feigning ignorance.

"Yeah, that's how Korean bathrooms are," Becky explained. "That's what the drain in the floor is for. To clean the bathroom, they just spray everything down, and everything goes down the drain." My next shower was unfettered, and I even purposefully splashed water everywhere, as if I were a little kid again playing in the bathtub. It was fun, liberating, and I began to wish bathroom cleanup was as simple and efficient back home.

Becky had already been to Korea and is fluent in Korean, so we had a slight leg up on our adventures, but still experienced some not-so-great treatment as American tourists. The day Becky and I went to search for my birth records, we had to take a cab to the children's hospital. Being from New York, we could hail a cab with the best and figured it wouldn't present any problems. A cab stopped, and the driver asked us where we wanted to go. When we told him it was the children's hospital, he quickly replied he didn't know where that was, and before we could explain, he drove away.

The second cabdriver to stop also rolled down the window and asked us what our destination was. Again, we told him the hospital, and like the first driver, he said he didn't know where it was and sped off before we could say anything. The situation curiously resembled trying to catch a yellow cab from Manhattan to Queens after a Broadway show or late dinner. Frustrated and feeling slighted as tourists, we settled on a new strategy.

When the third cab stopped, we opened the door and quickly got in. The driver started moving and asked us where we were headed. Almost expecting his reply, we told him the children's hospital, and as predicted, he acted confused and said he didn't know how to get there. This time Becky refused to take no for an answer. She got on her phone, dialed the hospital, and handed it to the driver. "Get directions," she demanded in Korean. "We're not going anywhere until you get directions and take us to the hospital." Taken aback by Becky's assertiveness, he took the phone, spoke with the person, and proceeded to take us to the hospital. Relieved that we were finally on our way, Becky broke the silence and explained to the driver why she pushed him so much. After hearing that two cabdrivers had rudely driven off, he apologized and tried to explain that it was lunch hour, and nobody wanted to go so far out of town. He was actually nice for the remainder of the trip and got us to the hospital without any further problems.

On another day of touring, Becky and I ended up in Itaewon, a popular shopping district that attracts throngs of tourists from all over the world. Many of the major hotels are in Itaewon, and it's known as a good place to buy souvenirs. We strolled in and out of shops, and as Becky stopped momentarily at a jewelry counter, the saleswoman began speaking to her in English. Although Becky is fluent in Korean, she replied back in English. The saleswoman pulled an amethyst pendant from the showcase and went right into her sales pitch. Because Becky spoke in such perfect English, the saleswoman must have just assumed she didn't understand Korean as what played out next indicated—much to our future amusement.

As the saleswoman continued about the beauty and quality of locally mined amethyst and how good it would look on Becky, a younger saleswoman from a neighboring booth approached and, in Korean, asked her colleague a question. The woman talking to Becky continued to look down, and without missing a beat, she quickly replied under her breath to the other woman. Neither of the saleswomen knew that Becky understood everything they said, and the situation became reminiscent of the *Seinfeld* episode when Elaine sent George's father into a nail salon to find out if the girls were making fun of her in Korean.

Becky ended up not buying the pendant, and as we left, she explained what happened. The younger saleswoman had asked the other one for change, and the older woman's reply translated loosely as "Are you crazy? How dare you interrupt me while I'm in the middle of a sale! I'll deal with you later." Becky is still amazed that she was able to keep a straight face through the whole thing.

All in all, there weren't too many culture shocks during the trip. Luckily, my time spent in rural Thailand prepared me for the in-ground toilet at a restaurant we ate at in an older part of Seoul. Like New York City, Seoul is urban and crowded in areas, but it's also much cleaner and orderly. There were also many pleasant surprises, including an immaculate public transportation system and food ordered for delivery comes on real dishes that the delivery person comes back later to pick up.

Another highlight was our visit to the Korean Folk Village, a historical theme park where visitors can get a taste of Korean culture and life during the late Joseon Dynasty (fourteenth to nineteenth centuries). We saw a reenactment of a traditional Korean wedding, saw how typical Koreans lived some two hundred years ago, and perhaps most importantly, we got to walk on the ground where parts of *Dae Jang Geum*, Becky's favorite Korean drama, was filmed.

*Becky with Dae Jang Geum at Korean Folk Village*

*Becky and me at the Korean Folk Village*

Before Becky and I got married, I had no idea what a Korean drama was. These various television series are loved by Koreans and are also highly popular in other parts of Asia. As a single male, this staple of life for many Koreans hadn't yet crossed my radar. I knew about American soap operas and mini series, but there's something special about the devotion among some to Korean dramas. After many years together, I can confidently say that Becky is the Korean drama queen. Okay, I'm sure this is a highly contested title among Korean women. Should the crown be awarded for total series watched? How about for most consecutive episodes or hours? There are many nights I've had to check who is sobbing in the next room—Becky or the actress in the drama. More often than not, it's both.

In all seriousness though, not all Korean dramas are over-the-top soap operas with sub-par acting and corny story lines. Becky has convinced me that certain dramas are useful for learning about Korean culture and history. Also, as I'm always trying to learn more Korean, hearing the language and reading subtitles is actually a helpful tool.

So far, the only one I've watched with any interest is *Dae Jang Geum*, a fictional story based on the life of an actual Joseon Dynasty palace cook who went on to become the first female royal physician. I've still only made it through half of the daunting fifty-four episodes. I promised Becky I would eventually finish it, and I'm sure she won't mind watching it again with me.

We were excited when we got to take our picture standing next to Jang Geum. Actually, it was a life-sized cardboard cutout of the famous actress who played the role, but we took what we could get.

Based on Korean history, though not completely accurate, dramas such as *Dae Jang Geum* are still worthwhile as something adoptive parents and Korean adoptees can watch together to learn more about Korean history, culture and language.

# COMMUNICATION IS CRITICAL
# WHEN YOU MARRY INTO A FAMILY

*Behind every successful man is a proud wife*
*and a surprised mother-in-law.*
*—Hubert H. Humphrey*

Ripostes about hypercritical, overly intrusive in-laws have become comedic clichés in sitcoms and stand up, but Becky and I both lucked out on the in-law front. Like all married couples, we didn't only become one with each other when we took our vows, we also became members of each other's families. In my case, this journey started well before our wedding day.

I moved to New York eight months before Becky and I got married and spent a lot of time with Becky's mom and her crew of Korean *ajummas* (married Korean women) while I adjusted to New York life and hunted for a job. Much of our time together was awkward as we could barely communicate, but she made me feel welcome in their home and took care of me from the day I arrived.

Becky's mom always kept me well fed, though sometimes to interesting ends. She often invited me to lunch with her friends, and I would eat in silence as she and her friends gossiped away in Korean. One day at home, she made tuna salad but realized she didn't have any bread. What she did have was a cake from the Korean bakery and proceeded to prepare a tuna on cake sandwich, which I couldn't refuse. Torn between guilt and preservation of my appetite, I snuck the sandwich into the garbage and covered it up with some papers after she left the room.

She also made me feel like my "Western wisdom" was valued—though sometimes to messy results. I learned that a lot of Korean-American families don't use their dishwashers to actually wash dishes, and essentially, the dishwasher amounts to a drying and storage rack. I kept questioning why they didn't use the dishwasher as it made cleanup easier, especially after big dinners like Thanksgiving.

So, late one night, Becky's mom decided to take my advice. It was about one a.m., and Becky and I had fallen asleep watching a movie on the couch. We awoke suddenly to Becky's mom yelling for us, and we bolted into the kitchen. There she stood in what looked like a giant bubble bath as more suds poured out of every side of the dishwasher onto the floor. "What happened?" Becky yelled. Her mom explained the steps she took, including filling the detergent cup with the soap sitting on the countertop—the liquid soap used for washing dishes in the sink.

We spent the next couple of hours starting the rinse cycle to flush the soap out of the dishwasher, mopping up the suds, and repeating until it was all cleaned up.

Most importantly though, Becky's mom accepted me for who I was. I was adopted, didn't speak Korean, and wasn't a doctor or lawyer. In fact, after leaving my job in Colorado to move to New York, I was an unemployed graduate student and drove a Dodge Neon. Despite all this, she accepted me as a son even before Becky and I were married.

Becky's dad wasn't as easily convinced in the beginning, but after years of sharing an office, he eventually became fond of having me around and now considers me a son. In that office, I heard a lot of stories, answered a lot of questions, and received a lot of advice.

At first, Becky's dad wasn't sold on my career change and decision to study and pursue a career in public relations. It's difficult enough to explain to members of my own generation exactly what I do for a living, and I could only best define PR as "kind of like marketing" to Becky's dad.

One day he sat me down for a talk about what I needed to do to become wealthy and successful. "You need to get a license. The only way to make money is if you have a license," he explained. "Doctors, certified public accountants, lawyers all have licenses," he added. I've only held two licenses during my life—driver's and fishing, but since I'm not on the NASCAR or Pro Bass circuits, I haven't cashed in from either. Despite his advice, I was set on PR, and the perceived prestige of me getting a master's degree from New York University ended up being good enough in the end.

Becky's dad also had concerns about me being adopted. Becky explained that it was less about me not knowing my Korean kin and more about what would happen if I ever met them. Coming directly from the Korean culture, Becky's dad knew all too well about the potential problems that would arise should I find my birth mom. Would she reject or not want to meet me? If she did accept me, would she expect financial support? These are all things I had thought of, but I was surprised that Becky's dad was also worried for me in this regard. Still, the simple fact that I was adopted didn't sit quite well with Becky's dad when she and I first met.

While pursuing my master's degree in public relations, I spent three straight years immersed in communication theory. The two-way symmetrical communication model asserts that successful communication flows from listening first and speaking second. People aren't inanimate objects that you speak at; instead, they react to messages with their own feelings, thoughts, fears, hopes, and dreams.

Understanding what moves individuals and groups to think or act in a certain way is paramount in cross-cultural communication. Good communicators must become what one of my professors described as social anthropologists in order to meet your audience on its own terms. This doesn't mean you must always agree with an opposing viewpoint, but if you don't at least acknowledge it and make an effort to understand its context, your audience won't even begin to listen to you.

These principles of cross-cultural communication often apply when a couple gets married and two families merge. A few years back, I read and replied to an advice column in *Adoptive Families Magazine* written about a nervous Korean woman waiting to introduce the man she loves and wants to marry to her parents. Already a nerve-wracking event, the situation was further complicated by the fact that her future husband is a Korean adoptee. This is my letter to the editor that the magazine published: "The transracial parenting expert's column really hit home. I'm a Korean adoptee who married into a traditional Korean family. My in-laws prefer speaking Korean, eat Korean food every day, and shop at Korean stores. My wife's family has accepted me as a son and brother, but, at first, my father-in-law was hesitant about his daughter marrying a non-Korean-speaking adoptee with an Irish last name. People of his generation still place a strong importance on bloodline and on speaking Korean. Korean adoptees that marry into traditional Korean families need to be aware of this, and I'm glad that my wife didn't hide it from me. It's easy to get offended by this way of thinking, but adoptees should be sensitive to the culture."

As a Korean adoptee, I believe it's only natural to be defensive about how some Koreans still view us. To be honest, in the past, I've often thought, *How dare you look down on us! It was your culture and society that gave us up to begin with!* This was usually a heat-of-the-moment thought after being criticized for not speaking Korean or knowing a custom, but I know not all Korean people think this way. In fact, as my letter concludes, I feel that adoptees should also be careful about judging. My father-in-law's generation is a product of its culture, just as much as I am of mine. Open, honest dialogue with Becky helped me deal with this issue. She made me aware of how my father-in-law initially felt, but more importantly, why he felt that way. For us, communication will only become more important, as per tradition, Becky's parents will eventually come to live with us.

My continuing research on Korean history and society has also aided in establishing my own cultural empathy. Becky and I have been married since 2005, and my in-laws see that their daughter is happy. This, above all, is the most important thing for them. For other parents, tradition may not subside so easily, but regardless, it's important to get these feelings out in the open. Ignoring them will only foster a lifetime of silent resentment.

# Rejecting Mom's Food is Trouble in Any Culture

*Food is our common ground, a universal experience.*
*—James Beard*

We weren't allowed to waste food when we were kids. You ate what you took and there wasn't such a thing as scraping your plate into the trash. If you didn't finish your food, you had to put it in the fridge and eat it for the next meal. Cold fried eggs for dinner? Meatloaf and peas for breakfast? You bet. When I was in second and third grade, I hated the lunches my mom packed. These were the days before those lunchbox ice packs, so a yogurt would be warm, and a banana mushy by noon. When you're a kid, all you want is PB&J on white bread, but my mom always made sandwiches on multigrain bread with seeds. So, there were many days that I would only eat half my lunch, or not at all.

Normally, I would have just thrown the food I didn't want in the lunchroom trashcans, but this wasn't allowed. At my elementary school in Billings, Montana, there were actually trashcan monitors that stood guard and made sure students only threw away trash, not food. With no way to dispose of the food I didn't want, my only choice was to keep it in my lunchbox. However, I knew I couldn't take the food back home, or I'd get in trouble. Being a resourceful kid, I found a creative solution.

My family became good friends with the next-door neighbors, and I would walk home with their daughter pretty much every day. It was half-a-mile between home and school, and we'd follow a standard route up one long street that lead to our back gates. There was a dog in the backyard of one of the houses we passed. That dog came to love me, as at the same time every afternoon, I'd toss my uneaten lunch items over the fence and into the yard for the mutt to gobble up. It was a perfect symbiotic relationship. The dog got a daily treat, and I got to get rid of the evidence that I hadn't eaten my lunch. My neighbor friend kept my secret and even helped me out on one occasion.

It was a yogurt day. I didn't eat it, and at some point during the day after lunch, the container exploded and filled my lunchbox with sour strawberry goo. I didn't even realize it until I opened my box on the way home. I was horrified. I knew I was busted this time. *What the heck am I going to do with this mess?* I asked myself. There was no throwing this over to the dog. I started to brainstorm. *Maybe I can hold the box over the fence and let the dog lick it clean,* I thought. "Oh man, I'm going to be in big trouble," I said to my friend.

"Don't worry, just come over to my house, and we'll figure it out," she reassured me.

We went through her back gate so we wouldn't have to pass the front of my house and possibly be spotted. We went into her kitchen, and her mom was there. My friend explained to her mom what happened and asked if she could wash out my lunchbox for me. Her mom cleaned up the mess, and I headed home relieved. Later in the afternoon, my friend and her mom came over to visit. Both of our moms chatted away in the kitchen, and I was petrified that her mom was going to spill the beans. I lurked around the kitchen listening for any mention of yogurt or lunchboxes. "What's wrong with you, Peter?" my mom asked. "Why are you acting so weird?"

"Uh, nothing," I replied nervously, praying the code of mothers wouldn't override keeping the secret of the neighbor kid. My friend's mom didn't tell, though, and I was safe after all.

School lunches aside, I liked my mom's cooking (and still do). Korean food was a treat in my family and something we reserved for special occasions. Yes, my German mom made Korean food, and it was something we all relished. Okay, to be fair, we ate dishes that are friendly to the American palate: *bap* (rice), *bulgogi* (Korean marinated beef), and fried *mandoo* (Korean dumplings). It's not like we stocked our pantry with dried squid and seaweed; kimchi was as adventurous as we got.

Rice and kimchi became a staple in my diet after I moved in with Becky's parents while she and I waited to close on our first home. As a kid, I couldn't imagine ever getting tired of Korean food, but I soon discovered it's possible. Don't get me wrong, I still enjoy it, but it's ironic when a bowl of Cheerios or Rice Krispies becomes a coveted treat.

During my first trip to New York to meet Becky, we went out to a Korean restaurant with her family and had a private dining room. "I can handle pretty much anything–except for fish with their head still on," I told Becky during one of our previous discussions about Korean food. The meal came in courses and seemed to never end. As luck would have it, the moment Becky left the table for the restroom, the waitress came in and set a plate of whole fish on the table. Without skipping a beat, Becky's mom grabbed one of the fish with her chopsticks and plopped it down on my plate. "Thank you," I said politely as I stared down at the fish, and it up at me. I stalled the best I could, munching on the things I felt comfortable with. After what seemed like an eternity, Becky walked back into room and our eyes locked as she saw the fish in front of me. She took her seat, took the plate away and started picking the fish apart and gave me the edible parts. Becky's mom said something in Korean that I didn't understand. "Mom said she was so impressed that I was serving you and taking such good care of you," Becky explained to me later. "She didn't know about you not being able to handle eating whole fish."

After I moved to New York, the time I spent living with my in-laws was an interesting culinary experience. As part of a generation of older Koreans, Becky's parents still prefer the traditional Korean breakfast of soup and rice. The first morning at my in-laws' house, I walked into the kitchen, and the unmistakable scent of something from the ocean hit my nostrils. "Good morning," I said to Becky's mom as I glanced nervously at the pot full of fish head soup.

"Good morning," she replied while she sampled the soup for flavor and added a dash of salt. "You eat breakfast," she said. She didn't speak with English inflection, so I wasn't sure if it was a question or a command. It could've been "You eat breakfast?" or "You. Eat breakfast."

"Okay," I said and figured my response would cover both. I sat down and braced myself as my mother-in-law placed a bowl of soup on the table. I tentatively tasted it. Not surprisingly it tasted like, well, fish. The broth was slightly salty and simply not something I was used to eating for breakfast.

"Good?" she asked, with an honest interest to make her son-in-law happy.

"Mmm, yes," I lied while I poked at the fish with my chopsticks like a five-year-old.

I stomached what I could, feigned a general lack of appetite, and excused myself. I then immediately called Becky at her family's business. "Honey, you have to tell Mom that I can't eat fish and soup for breakfast," I pleaded.

"Okay, okay," she agreed. "I'll talk to her."

A few days later, I came into the kitchen, and my mother-in-law was scrambling eggs. I thought to myself, *Thank God.*

That breakfast taught me something else about traditional Korean meals: you share *everything* on the table.

When I was a kid, meals at home were traditional American. We all sat down to individual settings and placed portions of food on our plates from larger dishes. If you wanted seconds, you took more with the serving utensil; you didn't dare stick your fork or spoon in the serving dish. The food on the plate in front of you was yours, and you finished what you took. So when Becky's mom placed a giant omelet in front of me, I assumed I was supposed to eat the whole thing. I didn't know that the space in front of me wasn't my space; it was simply available space.

Again, I didn't want to offend Becky's mom and not eat what she served me, so I dug in. Stuffed, I finally finished the entire thing, thanked my mother-in-law, and went to turn on my computer. "You there?" I typed into an instant message to Becky.

"What's up?" she messaged back.

"I appreciate that Mom doesn't feed me fish for breakfast anymore, but how much food does she think I eat?"

"LOL, what happened now?" Becky inquired.

"She made a huge omelet, and I ate the whole thing so I wouldn't be rude. She can't keep feeding me like this," I protested.

"Wait, Mom is calling me now," she typed.

From my room, I heard Becky's mom talking on the phone. I didn't understand any Korean at this point, so I had no idea what she was saying, but she sounded slightly annoyed.

*Oh great*, I thought to myself and feared Becky was ratting me out in an undiplomatic fashion.

A few minutes passed, and I started typing again. "What did Mom say?"

"You really want to know what she said?" Becky replied.

"Yes, of course, what did she say?" I prodded.

"This is exactly what she told me: 'I made a three-egg omelet for both of us to share, and that pig ate the whole thing!'"

Becky continued, "You better learn to communicate with your mother-in-law because I can't get involved in every little issue!"

Over the next couple of days, I convinced Becky's mom to let me handle my own morning meals. To my surprise, she actually seemed relieved.

I've become more adventurous with Korean food over the past six years. The fish heads don't totally freak me out anymore, and squid tentacles don't make me squeamish, but still, I'll stick with cereal for breakfast.

I probably should have mentioned that when I moved to New York, I was a pescetarian (a person who eats seafood but not other animals). I don't remember the exact moment I chose this; it was something I started when I moved to California after college, and it just stuck. It was mostly for health reasons and partially a moral decision. When it came to animal rights, I was never a zealot, but I've always had a strong affinity for animals. When I was a kid, we had a Moran family reunion at the beach in Delaware. One night we had fresh crabs for dinner, and

I remember the entire process disturbed me. First, we placed the live crabs into the freezer to slow them down. Once they couldn't pinch or claw, we dropped them one by one into a pot of boiling water. Anyone who has cooked crabs like this knows that the steam inside the shells escapes through the openings and creates a high-pitched whistling sound similar to a teapot. "I'm not eating any crabs," I told my mom.

"Why not?" she said, demanding an explanation.

"Because when you drop them in boiling water, I can hear them screaming," I explained with disapproval in the torture of the poor shellfish. Ironically, I was willing to eat hotdogs that night. When you're young, you don't really stop and think about where food like that comes from. After all, I wasn't the one who slaughtered the cow, the pig—and whatever else goes into a typical hotdog.

For two of my three years in California, I became a strict vegan. In the end, I gave it up after realizing the lifestyle was too hard to maintain without being a hypocrite. After all, the cow that provided the leather for my belt and shoes was just as dead as the one in a flame-broiled Whopper. I couldn't swing the all-hemp wardrobe, so I returned to eating seafood and decided it was strictly a health decision.

In the beginning, my mother-in-law hated the fact that I didn't eat meat because it made cooking more difficult. I'm still not completely convinced that she didn't sneak meat into some of my food, but regardless, I started to willingly eat meat again in the fall of 2005. I quickly rediscovered my love of Korean BBQ, and a few months later, as the whole family ate Korean short ribs, my mother-in-law said something, and everyone laughed.

"What?" I asked curiously.

Becky translated the blunt observation her mom just made. "Mom said she regrets encouraging you to eat meat."

"Why?" I asked, thinking she felt guilty for pushing me to abandon a decade-old lifestyle.

"Because, before you started to eat meat again, there was more for the rest of us."

# TRADITIONS CAN BE PAINFUL

*I've hired you to help me start a war. It's a prestigious line of work,*
*with a long and glorious tradition.*
—Vizzini, *The Pricess Bride*

T he musical *Fiddler on the Roof* opens with the rousing number
"Tradition," which is all about how family and religious
traditions define the people of Anatevka in 1905 Tsarist Russia.
Much like Jewish culture, traditional Korean life milestones are steeped
in ceremony, from a baby's first birthday (*dol*) to a grandparent's
funeral–and everything in between. Before I married Becky, most of my
knowledge of Korean traditions came from books, movies, and Korean
heritage camps. In fact, our wedding was the first time I experienced
traditional Korean ceremonies of any kind.

*Jeremy's first birthday (dol)*

Like many Korean-American weddings, ours was a fusion of Western and Eastern customs. My mom wore a *hanbok* (traditional Korean attire) for the lighting of candles with Becky's mom, and both our Korean and English ministry pastors translated the entire ceremony in both languages. I dislike being in the spotlight, so having to stand up in front of everyone for the ceremony in both languages was extra difficult.

After the reception dinner, our families were whisked away to partake in *Paebaek* (a traditional Korean bowing ceremony). Becky and I cut the cake, and we left the rest of the guests to enjoy their dessert and hit the dance floor as the DJ transitioned the tunes from Frank Sinatra to hip-hop. Like a couple of quick-change artists, Becky and I underwent a transition of our own, slipped into our *hanboks*, and headed into the *Paebaek* room where family and close friends waited.

*Paebaek* is rooted in the Korean tradition of a bride paying respect as the groom's parents accept her into the family. During the modern *Paebaek*, the bride and groom bow to relatives on both sides,

*Mom and Dad Lee during Paebaek Ceremony*

starting with the groom's family and ending with the bride's. It's also customary for parents and relatives to present the bride and groom with a small cash gift in a red envelope after receiving their bows. My family of course wasn't familiar with this, and Becky's dad kept reminding us to explain it so they wouldn't feel bad when they saw him doing it. It was awkward asking for gifts, especially money, but we explained the custom to my parents, and in turn, they told my aunts, uncles, and cousins.

We started by bowing to my parents and followed with my aunts, uncles, and cousins. Having been informed ahead of time at the repeated behest of Becky's dad, they had all prepared envelopes for us. When it came time for us to pay our respects to Becky's parents, we bowed, and after all the worrying and reminding, Becky's dad had forgotten to prepare his envelope. Trying to casually brush it off, he fumbled for the cash in his front pocket, pulled off the rubber band, and handed us a couple of wrinkled bills.

For *Paebaek*, the actual bowing is more elaborate than simply bending at the waist. The bride and groom start by standing, then the groom goes down on his knees, and the bride sits in a cross-legged position. In unison with hands folded, both bow their heads to the floor, rise up, and remain kneeling and sitting. This is repeated for all groups of family members. This is followed by a tea ceremony, giving of advice from parents, and the tossing of chestnuts and dates, which, depending on how

*Mom and Dad Moran tossing chestnuts and dates*

many the bride catches in her *hanbok*, symbolizes the number of girls and boys the couple will have.

Normally this wouldn't be a problem for me, but the week before, I had played soccer and ended up with a painful scab on my right knee. I spent most of the *Paebaek* smiling through gritted teeth while trying to shift most of my weight to my left knee. Every time we bowed, I had to distribute my weight evenly and was relieved when we were done and I could stand again. I didn't know it at that point, but the night still had more pain in store.

There's a Korean post-wedding ceremony custom that involves the groom lying on his back and the bride's relatives and friends hold his legs upright and take turns beating the soles of his feet with a stick. Everyone told me that the practice originated from a symbolic way of making it too painful for a groom to abandon his wife on the wedding night and run away. Regardless of how it began, it seems to have evolved into a fraternity-style initiation and a way for the guys to test how much pain the groom can endure.

Having lived through this painful ordeal, I became curious about other bizarre wedding traditions from around the world, and in my research, I discovered it could be worse. Traditionally, the Tidong, a native people of Borneo, are prohibited from using the bathroom for three days and nights after getting married. Their family monitors the couple closely to make sure the rule isn't broken, and failure is considered bad luck for the marriage. I couldn't find anything to confirm that it's still commonly practiced, but given the choice between this and feet beating, I'll endure temporarily sore feet anytime. Yes it hurts like hell, but I love coffee and my Saturday *New York Times* way too much to endure the former.

# LANGUAGE IS A FUNNY THING

*Come, let us go down and confuse their language so*
*they will not understand each other.*
*—Genesis 11:7, NIV*

Several years back, I was at a friend's house watching a football game. At one point, the couple's four-year-old son captivated me as he effortlessly used a laptop to play games and watch videos. I stretched my memory back to 1979 and tried to remember what technology I was using at age four. Frankly, I couldn't remember, but I guessed at most it was a typewriter. Now, I watch my own son, Jeremy zip through apps on an iPad.

As a member of Generation X, I witnessed the rise of e-mail, instant messaging, cell phones, texting, and social media. We can easily trace the origins of these communication tools: Most of them evolved from existing technologies through human innovation.

Unlike these media vehicles we communicate through, the thing we communicate *with* has a much fuzzier past. The origin of human language still puzzles scientists, linguists, and historians. There are many widely discussed theories but no absolute consensus on how human language arose or, for that matter, how our capacity for language even exists.

Before I moved to New York City, I never gave much thought to language. Sure, I took a couple years of Spanish in high school, but everyone I communicated with on a daily basis spoke English.

After I married into a family where everyone speaks fluent Korean, I started to think a lot more about language and how people view it. It's interesting how our frame of reference rests on our native language.

For example, I might ask Becky, what is rabbit in Korean? In the same way, a Korean person learning English would ask, what is *to-ki* in English? I admit, it's easy to become self-centered regarding language, but as a Korean in Flushing who doesn't speak Korean, I've often experienced language prejudice.

I've gone through the same routine with Korean bank tellers, taxi drivers, grocery store clerks, deli owners, and church members. Because of the way some communities have developed in New York, many immigrants can live in a certain section and never really have to learn or speak English. So, because I'm Korean and fall within a certain age range, other Koreans automatically assume I speak the language. When someone realizes I don't speak Korean, he or she often poses a statement phrased as a question. "Oh, you're not Korean," to which I always reply, "Yes, I'm Korean."

"So you were born in the United States then?" and I retort, "No, I was born in Korea." At this point, he or she usually looks completely confused, and I sometimes let them flounder for a moment before I clear up the issue with my limited Korean. "Woori um-munee geureego abuhjee neun hangook saram ahnee aeyo," which means "My parents aren't Korean." I follow up with "I'm adopted," and this last part usually elicits an acknowledgement of "Oh, I see" and quickly draws the conversation to a close. Most of these exchanges are awkward but pleasant. Every so often though, someone will question my lack of Korean speaking with an implied accusatory tone.

More than twenty years ago, my father-in-law bought a wholesale beauty supply company, and since then, the family has distributed manicure and pedicure supplies to nail salons all around the world. I joined the company and worked alongside Becky and her dad for nearly five years before I went into public relations.

Most of their New York customers speak primarily Korean, which often made even the simple task of answering the phone an exercise in futility.

The business hosts an annual trade show where a variety of companies come to display and sell their products. During the years

I've worked at the show, many Korean nail salon workers have expressed their impatience at my lack of Korean speaking. It's as if they think, "How dare you be Korean and not speak the language!" Dealing with occasional attitudes like this is part of my love-hate relationship with the culture. Over the years, I've become more comfortable letting Koreans know I don't speak Korean. I don't let a negative or surprised reaction bother me. I've also realized that my experience isn't exclusive to adoptees. I have many Korean American peers that have Korean parents but don't speak fluent Korean. Some grew up speaking Korean at home, others didn't.

At some point, I may learn enough Korean to communicate fluently. However, as I get older, I'll be increasingly surrounded by generations of Koreans who grew up speaking as much—if not more—English than Korean. That said, I admit I've had fun improving my basic Korean from watching a cartoon called *Pororo* with Jeremy. Nothing beats the pride of actually understanding what the animated penguin is talking about to the polar bear, dinosaur, and his other friends.

# TIME HEALS BOTH SKINNED KNEES
## AND BRUISED EGOS

*Stereotypes do exist, but we have to walk through them.*
*—Forest Whitaker*

When I was a kid, school playgrounds were veritable arenas of asphalt, steel, and wood. These were the days before school administrators padded the blacktop, and foursquare had nothing to do with becoming "mayor" of the local Starbucks. We played dodge ball, red rover, and anything else that involved hurtling big rubber balls or ourselves at each other. If we fell and skinned a knee, we got up and scrambled for our lives.

Okay, it wasn't a complete war zone; we occasionally let our guards down to trade "friendship pins" for our shoelaces and watch the fifth graders breakdance on flattened cardboard boxes. However, my schoolyard cohorts passed around more than safety pins filled with colored beads and the latest backspin technique. Once or twice a week, the grapevine would produce the latest dirty joke or limerick; you know, stuff first and second graders don't fully understand but laugh at anyway so as not to look stupid.

Two of the milder "poems" stuck in my memory.

"Me Chinese, me play joke, me put pee-pee in your Coke," the kids would chant, along with "Chinese, Japanese, dirty knees, look at these!" Motions where kids would slant their eyes up and down, touch their knees, and cup the air in front of their chest to show off a pair of imaginary large breasts accompanied this one.

We just repeated what our older siblings and classmates heard and passed down. In fact, I'm not self-righteous enough to claim I didn't repeat these jokes and laugh with everyone else. Was it because I was too young to know better? Was it because I grew up "white," and the stereotypes didn't sting as much as they would have had I grown up in a Korean family? Was I just too stupid to realize I was making fun of myself? I'm sure it was a bit of all of the above. It wasn't until high school that Asian stereotypes actually hurt my ego.

During sophomore year, my school's drama club performed Cole Porter's *Anything Goes*. That night was the first time I suddenly became self-conscious in public about being Asian. This classic musical, which takes place on an ocean liner en route from New York to England, features two Chinese characters named Ching and Ling. I still remember sinking into my seat, angry and embarrassed as I watched two of my white classmates shuffle on stage wearing bamboo hats, squint their eyes, and deliver their lines in a typical mock Asian accent. The only way it could have been worse is if they had pulled up the corners of their eyes with their fingers or been wearing fake buckteeth.

"We no lose. We *win*! Three hundred dollar."

They continued their act as the audience snickered, which only added to my humiliation as an Asian American.

In all fairness, Porter wrote the musical in 1934, well before mainstream society cringed at racial stereotypes. Still, at that moment, nothing mattered to me except a theater full of people laughing at Ching and Ling, and I'm Korean, not Chinese.

As I look back on my embarrassment and anger, perhaps I overreacted. However, for the 1987 Broadway revival of the musical, the playwright replaced Ching and Ling with new characters named Luke and John. This was a few years before I got to high school, but it proves I wasn't the only one who felt Ching and Ling's kitschy antics had run their course.

My views on race were formed over time, and growing up, I had some naive views and understandings about race relations in the U.S. There was a time when I thought that racism was something that only white people could have against minorities. One day when my parents were away, I ended up watching Spike Lee's *Do The Right Thing*, and it had a real impact on me. I had no idea the extent of the racial tensions that existed between different minority groups. Living in white suburbia doesn't really expose one to such realities. Three years later, the 1992 Los Angeles riots that followed the Rodney King trial really broke my heart. It wasn't because I saw a clash of races as I watched armed storeowners defending their property in Koreatown—it was because I saw people of all colors using the legitimate topic of race to justify criminal behavior.

My sensitivities seemed slightly off one way or another at different ages, but as an adult, I now see everything in context. Years back, Becky and I attended a Subway Series Game, which is what it's called when the Mets play the Yankees. The game was at Shea Stadium before they tore it down and built Citi Field. We were walking up the stadium ramp to our section, and not far behind us was a group of guys who had obviously been tailgating all afternoon.

"Go, Mets!" they chanted in unison. Becky, being a Yankees fan, turned and retorted, "Go, Yankees!"

One of them then yelled, "Hey, look. It's Matsui's wife!"

Hideki Matsui is the Japanese-born MLB designated hitter and outfielder and at that time played for the Yankees. Becky and I laughed, and I was actually more honored than insulted. Sure, I wasn't making $13 million a year to hit a ball, but I took his alcohol-induced wit in stride.

While I find it difficult to stomach blatant racism, I'm now able to laugh at the stereotypes I'm supposed to fit as an Asian American. Political correctness can go too far, and there are simply some people that are ignorant but essentially harmless. Granted, it's easier for adults to accept this, and I understand that many kids *are* harmed emotionally by insensitive racial comments. I don't discount that. Bullying is a big problem in our schools, whether it's racially based or otherwise. However, I didn't have it so bad and just as the scrapes on my knees from falling on the playground have healed over time, I'm happy to say, my ego has too.

# IT'S IMPORTANT TO FACE YOUR FEARS

*"The oldest and strongest emotion of mankind is fear, and the oldest
and strongest kind of fear is fear of the unknown.*
—H. P. Lovecraft

I still have vivid memories of things that frightened me as a kid. A lot of my worst scares arose as movie and book villains converged with an overactive imagination. For instance, when I was three or four, my dad took my older sister and me to see *Star Wars*, and I was certain that Darth Vader was going to walk out of the screen and start killing people. I also recall being six and lying petrified in bed after seeing the 1981 movie *Clash of the Titans* as images of Medusa's snake-filled head appeared on and off in my bedroom's textured ceiling.

Other fears arose while learning how to swim. When my family lived in Minneapolis, my older sister and I took swimming at a nearby lake. At an age when I didn't understand the difference between freshwater and saltwater creatures, I was convinced the denizens that lurked in Lake Harriet included swarms of bloodthirsty sharks just waiting to snack on little boys and girls like floating pieces of popcorn shrimp. Even a couple years later at the YMCA, I remember being afraid to jump off the diving board into the deep end and hiding in the locker room through half the lesson.

However, the pièce de résistance of my childhood fears came while reading the book *It* when I was eleven or so. I was in bed late one night, deeply immersed and unable to put down Stephen King's classic horror novel when nature called. The bathroom was right across the hall from my bedroom, but as I reckoned, traversing even that short distance in the dark still provided the opportunity for Pennywise the clown to reach out from under the bed, grab my leg, and drag me into some evil netherworld.

I finally summoned the courage to dart across the hall and conduct my business, but once in the bathroom, I was sure I'd never make it back to my room alive, so there I sat, watching and listening to the clock's second hand, knowing I was safe in the confines of the well-lit bathroom—*tick, tick, tick*. Thirty minutes passed, then an hour. I eventually came to terms with the absurdity of camping out in the bathroom all night and finally summoned the courage to go back to my room. I opened the door just a crack and peered out into the hall. Then, like pulling off a Band-Aid as fast as possible to get it over with, I turned off the light and ran back into my room and jumped safely in bed. After that night, I only continued reading the book during daylight hours.

As an adult, my fears are more reality based, but in many cases are just as irrational. Then again, most fears are not based on reason, which is exactly what makes them so hard to face.

Throughout life, my adoption has elicited many feelings: curiosity, sadness, anger, pride, and camaraderie, but only one facet ever made me withdraw and close up. Only one produced fear.

Although Becky and I were raised quite differently, the value of family is something that runs deep through both of us. Throughout the process of starting our own family, I had to face and internalize a fear of bringing my life as an adoptee full circle by considering becoming an adoptive parent. It's something Becky brought up several times after losing Elijah, Luke, and Isabelle, but I always avoided talking about it. In the past, any time that Becky brought up the possibility of adoption I would get uncomfortable. It was something I didn't want to think about.

Many other adoptees have faced this life decision. I've heard from adopted friends who happily went on to adopt and others who are adamantly against it. A natural assumption would be for me to have no fears or reservations about adopting a child. My parents raised me to understand, embrace, and celebrate my adoption, and I can cite firsthand the blessings and benefits adoption affords so many children. On the other hand, I also know the hardships and heartache that many adoptive families face.

I was never completely against adopting, but I also desired to have a biological child and, for some reason, believed that would always happen first. I've learned the lesson in my heart that families are defined by love, not genes, but it wouldn't be honest for me to say my fears about adopting didn't include not knowing if I would at any point—even for a split second—view an adopted child differently than a biological child, or if that child would ever consider me anything less than his or her *real* father. I've openly admitted to Becky and others that the longing to see my own flesh and blood was rooted in ego. Perhaps it's selfish human nature, or maybe it's societal.

Whatever the reason, I can honestly say I've now opened my mind and heart to the possibility of adopting a child. I don't know if we'll decide to do it, but it remains a possibility. Yes, it's easier for me to discuss, say, after having Jeremy, but I can still envision myself holding an adopted son or daughter in my arms for the first time. In my mind's eye, I smile as the fear and selfish pride melts away. At that moment, the circle of my adoption story is complete, and for the next generation, a new one begins.

# Parting Thoughts

The most important lesson I've learned as an adoptee is that there are two sides to every tale. My adoption story is merely one recounted in the minds, writings, and conversations of an estimated 160,000 children adopted from South Korea since 1955. Behind this global collection of unique narratives lies a multiplicity of voices that don't always speak in unison.

One must reflect on the background of the Korean War to fully appreciate the issues of South Korean adoption. On June 25, 1950, communist North Korean troops poured across the 38th parallel and thrust the peninsula into a bitter three-year conflict. As in all war, children were the most tragic victims of what Dean Acheson, Secretary of State from 1949-1953, called "a sour war." The war caused millions of Korean and non-Korean military and civilian deaths and created an estimated 100,000 South Korean orphans.

In 1955, a film about Korean orphanages inspired Harry and Bertha Holt, an evangelical Christian couple from rural Oregon, to adopt eight Korean War orphans. Their radical decision singlehandedly popularized the concept of intercountry and transracial adoption. The story garnered national media coverage and over the following years, the Holts helped facilitate hundreds of proxy adoptions for other America families.

Although publicity was largely positive, various adoption professionals and policy-makers criticized the Holts for "threatening child welfare by substituting zeal and haphazard methods for professional skill and supervision."

During the 1970s and 80s, negative media coverage began to erode South Korea's adoption legacy and national reputation. It was North Korea's media that first began to openly criticize South Korea's intercountry adoptions.

South Korea's intercountry adoption peaked mid-1980s with nearly 9,000 children adopted internationally in 1985. Criticism of the continued volume of South Korean intercountry adoptions reached a head in 1988. As worldwide media descended on Seoul for the Summer Olympics, major outlets began to cover South Korea's intercountry adoption. NBC's Bryant Gumbel sparked negative coverage with his live interview comment that "babies seemed to be South Korea's primary export commodity." The *New York Times* and others followed—most memorably, the *Progressive*, which published an article titled, "Babies for Sale: South Koreans Make Them, Americans Buy Them."

During the late 1980s and 90s, humiliated by negative headlines, South Korea moved quickly to enact policies aimed to reduce and eventually eliminate intercountry adoption. The country didn't meet its goal to end all intercountry adoption by 1995. However, since 1986, the number of children adopted from South Korea has steadily decreased. In 1997, South Korea announced with fanfare that more South Korean children were adopted domestically than internationally that year. Despite this, some contend the number of Korean babies adopted overseas is still too high (approximately 1,065 in 2008 and 1,080 in 2009).

In 2008, rumors began to crop up on various online adoption sites hinting that South Korea once again aimed to end all intercountry adoptions by 2012, and it was even reported in a 2009 *New York Times* article. Some people refuted this, including individuals in South Korea familiar with South Korean adoption policy, and it's unclear whether or not South Korea is actively pursuing its goal to completely close the doors on intercountry adoptions.

Over the years, I've gotten to know dozens of Korean adoptees—young and old—and realized that intercountry adoption often polarizes the South Korean adoptee community. Many adoptees firmly believe they've received a much better life than their birth parents could have provided. Others harbor deep resentment against the country that gave them up and feel that adoption robbed them of their true identity. Some want to avert criticism or avoid appearing ungrateful to their adoptive parents and remain reluctant to express any feelings one way or another.

Many South Korean adoptees and adoption experts I've spoken with agree that completely ending South Korea's intercountry adoption is currently neither realistic nor viable. As for the future, opinions differ as to what this would require, or if it would be in the best interest of South Korean "orphans," whom most often are babies born out of wedlock and relinquished—not orphans in the classic sense of the word.

Something adoptees from any countries share is the unavoidable reality of a dual heritage. At some point in life, many South Korean adoptees are forced to ask themselves what it means to be a "real" Korean and reconcile their disparate ethnic and cultural identity—all without marginalizing their own adoption or positioning themselves as a victim.

South Korea's complex intercountry adoption issues continue to weave an intricate pattern of history and culture into the nation's social fabric. One of the biggest internal challenges to face South Koreans is the back-and-forth pull between modern and historical ideologies. Despite South Korea's younger, more progressive generations, Confucian principles of paternal bloodline and racial purity remain etched in the Korean psyche.

Although the South Korean government and people have taken many steps to address social and cultural norms, such as the stigma against single mothers and domestic adoption, there is still a lot of progress to be made.

By its very nature, intercountry and domestic adoption will continue to be pressing and controversial issues for South Korea and its people. Only time will tell to what extent internal attitudes and policies will change. Like Tevye's daughters in *Fiddler on the Roof*, South Korea's future generations that openly embrace new ideas and behaviors will face resistance from others that hold adamantly to custom and family tradition. In these instances of change, whether it's for better or worse is always a matter of perspective. However, for South Korea, I hope what's best for its children and society will ultimately prevail.

# ACKNOWLEDGMENTS

I owe many people thanks and gratitude for making this book a reality. This project would have never been possible without my wife, Becky, who supported me during many long nights of writing, helped me recall several details throughout the process, and gave honest feedback as each new section emerged. Remembering together was one of the best parts of writing this book.

I'd like to thank my parents for opening up their hearts and home thirty-seven years ago, and my brother and sisters and every family member that has touched my life since. This book is as much about and for you all as it is for me.

I'm also grateful for all of the adoptees I've come to know and befriend throughout my life. At its core, this book is about family and friends, and I've been blessed with the many people that are a part of these shared memories and experiences.

Special thanks to Jay Rubin, whose mentorship and friendship helped me become a better writer, as well as Jane Myung Park and Malia Jansson, who were kind enough to read through early manuscript drafts of this book and provide me with frank and invaluable suggestions.

Also, thanks to Nancy Pappas, a fellow Korean adoptee for taking on the cover design project. I was her counselor at Korean Heritage Camp, and she's one of the most talented artists and designers I know.

As this book began as a blog, I'd also like to thank everyone that followed Adoptee Voice and whose ongoing comments and interaction inspired me to keep writing and share bits and pieces of my adoption story.